Strength to Deliver®

How to Revive and Give Birth to Your Interrupted Dreams

Tolu Adeleye, Ph.D.

Strength to Deliver®: How to Revive and Give Birth to Your Interrupted Dreams

Copyright © 2012 by Tolu Adeleye, Ph.D.
Contemporary Lifestyle Publishing Inc.

All rights reserved. No part of this publication may be reproduced, stored in a retrieval system, or transmitted in any form or by any means, electronic, mechanical, photocopying, recording, or otherwise—other than for "fair use" as brief quotations embodied in articles and reviews—without the prior written permission of the publisher.

The author of this book does not dispense medical advice or prescribe the use of any technique as a form of treatment for physical, emotional or medical problems without the advice of a physician, either directly or indirectly. The intent of the author is only to offer information of a general nature to help you in your quest for emotional and spiritual well-being. The author disclaims liability for any adverse effects resulting directly or indirectly from information contained in this book.

ISBN: 978-1-936001-37-8

Also by Tolu Adeleye, Ph.D.

Stay Sane Through Change: How to Rise Above the Challenges of Life's Complex Transitions

Sanity and Strength: Wisdom to Get Unstuck and Power to Move on from the Muddy Paths of Life Transitions

Stay Sane Through Change® Series

In loving memory of my father,
Samuel Oludare Ogunbayo

Table of Contents

Chapter 1: Introduction 1

Chapter 2: The Lens of the Dreams' Midwife 9
    A unique view of the journey

Chapter 3: Strength at Various Levels 27
    An upfront review of your dreams fulfillment history

Chapter 4: Strength and Purpose 51
    Why it is important to re-consider your interrupted dreams

Chapter 5: Strength to Revive 75
    Breathing new life into your interrupted dreams

Chapter 6: Strength to Conceive 97
    Re-starting naturally or by means of assistance

Chapter 7: Strength to Grow 117
    Working towards proper development of your dream

Chapter 8: Strength to Protrude 139
    Managing extreme growth of your dream

Chapter 9: Strength to Bring Forth 159
    Releasing your dream to the world

Chapter 10: Strength to Celebrate 179
   Taking ownership of your newly delivered dream

Chapter 11: Strength to Provide 201
   Nurturing your newly delivered dream

Chapter 12: Strength to Multiply 221
   Reproducing your dream fulfillment

Chapter 13: Strength to Deliver 241
   Becoming an all-round dream achiever

Chapter 14: Creating a Ripple Effect 263
   Equipping others to find the strength to deliver

Notes 269

CHAPTER 1

Introduction

THE CLOGGED WHEEL

When I set out to write this book, I was living out one of my dreams. I saw this book as a major goal towards fulfilling my dream to move forward in my newly re-defined career of life coaching. I saw it as an appropriate resource to help stirring or evoking excellence in others. That was one of my uppermost thoughts at that time. In the previous six months before I started writing, I had been through a training which involved the sharing of coaching techniques with a wide variety of like-minded people. We were all professionals who had worked previously in other careers but desired to launch or re-solidify a career in coaching.

Towards the end of the course, I took several marketing initiatives designed to promote my life coaching business to a client niche that I had always wanted to work with. I have always had passion for people going through mid-life transitions, particularly those who have had life-changing experiences in their family and/or careers. I went through all of the necessary actions such as creation of marketing materials, hosting a business building teleseminar, and the introduction of special pages for coaching services in my main website.

Then all of a sudden, many issues in my life seemed to come to a standstill. In fact, it seemed the wheels that controlled the movement of events were desperately clogged and stuck in neutral. The wheels could neither move forward nor backward. I tried all I could to help 'unblock' the system. I went through a business-building course that lasted three months. That did not make much of a difference. As a matter of fact, the wheels became definitely grounded.

Then, I had a series of breakthrough changes in my situation. I realized I was able to focus on one major goal that was part of a forward movement. I directed my efforts towards that goal, while studying for the final exam of the coaching course. The process of studying for that exam effected more breakthroughs for me. As I read through the course work, I began to perceive many areas in my life to which these principles could apply. It was as if a light broke through.

This wonderful experience continued through to the week that I actually sat for the exams and even long afterward. When I finished the exam, I had a great sense of joy and release flowing through my entire being. I felt assured that I was now heading in the right direction and that was something magnanimous considering the events of the previous months!

A NEW REVELATION

During this turn of events, I had a dream about being involved in an organization that helps people birth their dreams. I instantly liked the idea, more so because it was so near the time I had interactions

• INTRODUCTION •

with different coaching professionals. I felt on top of the world and greatly motivated to put my pen to paper and write.

I have since embraced and further developed the idea. I have become a dream's midwife, passionate about the role I now play in bringing dreams to reality in the lives of others. But, the rest of my inspiration story continues below.

With this new light, I started drafting new concepts that were coming so rapidly to me. This sense of release and revelation was so great that I did not even have time to worry about the book series on which I had previously planned to work. This series was to follow the first book I co-authored—*Stay Sane Through Change*. This new revelation was so momentous; I could not walk away from it. So, step by step, I started putting together the first draft.

STRENGTH TO DELIVER: THE CONCEPT

In an interesting story in the Bible, a Hebrew king named Hezekiah was faced with a terribly challenging situation (1). His kingdom had been summoned to battle by another influential king—the king of Assyria. The battle was a crucial one because it would affirm the position of Israel as a force to be reckoned with among all of the surrounding nations. Prior to this, Israel had won many other victories over the other nearby nations. However, the kingdom of Assyria had been a threat to Israel for a long time. If Hezekiah lost the battle, the whole nation of Israel would be taken captive by Assyria and that was a prospect not easily contemplated. Losing that battle would plunge all of the other previous years of victory and expansion of the Israeli kingdom into nothingness. Thus, the battle was vital to the continuing prosperity of Israel as a nation.

However, the challenge by the Assyrian king came at a time when Hezekiah had no army to speak of ready to face a worthy enemy in such an important battle. Hezekiah was so confounded that he compared his situation to that of an expectant mother whose due date for giving birth had arrived but had no 'strength to deliver'. What a terrible dilemma!

In the past, I have often wondered about the predicament that this story relates. I have been fascinated by the phrase 'strength to deliver' for a long time. However, my wonder turned to reality when the wheels of my life seemed permanently clogged. I encountered a situation similar to that pregnant woman, whose baby was due, but had no strength to bring it forth.

I easily identified with the concept of the story. In the previous months, I had worked hard and gathered all resources towards giving birth to the vital dream I had borne in my womb for a time. Yet, when it was time to push to bring the baby forth, there were too many obstacles that obstructed the flow of events.

A WELL OF INSPIRATION

In a new way, I understood how important it is to have the strength to bring forth when the due date for birthing one's dream arrived. This fact, coupled with my vision of a 'dream-birthing' organization, gave me more motivation to work on the title *Strength to Deliver*.

At the beginning, I focused on a subtitle that would show how to overcome obstacles, which prevent you from birthing your dreams. However after initial work in this direction and more market surveys, it became clear that there are many people who previously abandoned vital dreams but are currently seeking to revive and realize them.

• INTRODUCTION •

It became more realistic and relevant to endeavour to remove obstacles that prevent you from birthing your dream. However, that aspect is just one of the many issues faced by a large number of people. For someone who started working on a vital dream, and who is faced with an interruption, the pressing issue is how to revive the dream after being inactive for a length of time. Such an individual has a different perception of the process of birthing a dream when compared to someone who is attempting to reach that same goal for the first time.

What's more, this theme resonates with the big picture of my personal experience. Launching a life-coaching career was part of a bigger legacy dream on which I had been working for a long time already. However, I have had many interruptions on the way towards fulfilling this particular legacy dream.

Taking a cue from the above, I changed my working subtitle and directed this book towards you, the person seeking to realize an important dream, which you previously abandoned.

COME ABOARD THE JOURNEY

Strength to Deliver is about reviving, re-vitalizing and birthing. It's about picking up your abandoned life goals, aligning them with your current life situation by re-conceiving them. It's about growing your re-conceived dream as you take new action-steps. It's about protruding and stretching your actions until you ultimately give birth to those dreams. It equips you to overcome the obstacles at different growth-stages of your dream. It empowers you to use new periods of interruption to your advantage. It gears you towards ensuring safe delivery of your previously interrupted dream the second time around.

In Chapter 2, we will review the dream delivery process from conception to birth using pregnancy and childbirth imagery. The next few chapters focus on assessing your interrupted dream in the light of your current position in life. We will discuss what it takes to breathe new life into that abandoned dream while clarifying with you what you really want in life.

In the chapters that follow, we will also discuss how to re-conceive your dream in the light of your present day circumstances and how to manage the growth of your dream from conception to delivery. I have illustrated the different possible points of interruption of the dream and the challenges you may face at each stage of growth. We will also discuss how to ensure that your dream does not get aborted inadvertently.

The last sets of chapters focus on nurturing your dream after you bring it forth, taking ownership of it so that the benefits spill into other areas of your life.

We will also discuss how to multiply your fulfillment by conceiving more dreams and repeating the whole cycle.

The book is interspersed with exercises designed to assist you in applying the concepts to your own situation. In addition, it contains copious examples taken from the lives of people like you who faced interruptions in their dreams, but revived and realized them later in life. These people belong to a wide range of classes and culture and live in different parts of the globe. Their dreams were as diverse in categories as career, health, relationship, spiritual, personal development, legacy, business, financial and leisure. I am quite sure their stories will inspire and motivate you.

• **INTRODUCTION** •

This book will:
- Empower you to recharge your zest for life
- Help you to discover new strength to deliver your previously abandoned dreams
- Equip you with a renewed sense of purpose and mission in life
- Help you to acquire a sense of fulfillment as you use the concepts to multiply your realized goals.

'Strength to Deliver' has been a journey for me. It is a paradox that putting this book together has actually helped me birth the dream that I knew was due for delivery at that time when I faced numerous obstacles. It has helped me to birth even many more dreams in the process of working on the major interrupted ones.

__Come aboard the journey!__

CHAPTER 2

The Lens of the Dreams' Midwife

A unique view of the journey

THE DREAMS' MIDWIFE

In my capacity as a 'dreams' midwife', my role is to help people revive their previously interrupted dreams as well as conceive new ones. In addition, my mission is to guide and support people through the period of their dream pregnancy and empower them through the delivery and post-natal process. I translated the childbirth imagery into the coaching process.

But that imagery of childbirth has been impressed upon me in other ways prior to that vision. In fact, I previously experienced a number of life-changing events that brought the imagery of childbirth closer to my heart.

One of those events was the birthing of my third child—a beautiful baby girl born the same week that I lost my mother. It was a very challenging situation. I became motherless four days after I became a mother for the third time. As I recall, my moment of great joy was mixed with a deep moment of grief. What a paradox! One of my main sources of comfort during these almost concurrent events was the fact that my mother would have loved to see her new grand-daughter raised properly. My mother would love for me to cherish the gift of new life that was given to me at the time of her passing. She would desire that I grasp that legacy of motherhood; the ability to nurture, provide and raise a daughter. At that time, the recognition of this fact gave me some empowerment. I will always cherish that legacy.

Another imagery of childbirth that I have had in more recent years was at the beginning of the writing of my first co-authored book. I had the vision that I was pregnant with the book-writing concept and that it was a dream that was due for delivery. What seemed pressing about the dream was the idea of co-authoring the book with F. David Webster, whom I had met through my home church. I did not understand why I should be writing a book with him at that particular point in time. However, I recognized the fact that the imagery I had received through the dream demanded somewhat an immediate decision. It was the imagery of a baby due to be born that struck me as urgent; and I went for it wholeheartedly. It was time to push and bring forth that dream. So I went through a process of translating my 'sleep dream' into a dream that I conceived in my active state of consciousness. I set new goals towards birthing the dream and worked hard to realize them. That first book entitled *Stay Sane Through Change* (1) was released nine months after my child birth 'sleep dream'.

My latest experience with the *Strength to Deliver* analogy has complemented the previous child birth imagery. My new experience has motivated me to embrace the concept of helping people in discovering the strength to deliver their dreams all the more.

I have become passionate about my role as the life coach who is the dreams' midwife. So, why don't you join the dreams' midwife on a kaleidoscopic tour of the dream delivery process?

PREGNANCY AND CHILDBIRTH: A PROCESS SUMMARY

In order to view that dream process kaleidoscope, I propose to guide you through a concise review of pregnancy and childbirth.

A woman conceives new life in her womb when her egg (ovum) has been fertilized. This new growth is the starting point of the amazing miracle of the new baby that is scheduled for delivery about nine months after the moment of conception.

The whole period of growth—the gestation period—is divided into three trimesters. Each trimester, as the name implies, lasts for about three months.

During the first trimester, the mother goes through tremendous changes in her body and hormone levels as the foetal cells divide at an incredible rate. Physical symptoms, such as morning sickness and breast tenderness, are hallmarks of this period. By the end of the first trimester, the baby has a heartbeat and can move his or her tiny arms and legs. The first trimester is the stage during which a mother is most prone to miscarriages or spontaneous loss of the foetus (2).

The second trimester of pregnancy is filled with more growth of the baby. As the pregnancy becomes better established, the early discomforts that the mother experienced during the first trimester gradually disappear. The uterus becomes larger and the pregnancy may become obvious to onlookers. However, the uterus is not yet large enough to make every activity uncomfortable. This stage is exciting as the mother can begin to feel the baby's movements.

In the third trimester of pregnancy, the baby grows rapidly and gains substantial weight. This results in protrusion of the abdomen, which, in turn, makes every activity more challenging. It becomes more difficult to find a comfortable sleeping position. The expectant mother experiences more minor contractions at this stage.

When the baby is due, the mother goes through a period of intensive contractions, appropriately termed, "labour". This process hails the bringing forth of the baby as the cervix dilates and 'the birth canal is opened up'. With enduring and painful pushes and in between breathing, the mother goes through the long-awaited birthing of her baby.

Most expectant mothers dream of delivering their baby safely. In fact, having children is a common dream among couples. Many people desire to have offspring and put this family dream as one of their priorities in life.

But what are dreams really?

WHAT DREAMS ARE

Dreams, in the context of this book, are what people conceive as their visions of an ideal future. So, someone who dreams of having children sees that event as an ideal place in their future. They envision a future of raising children and living together as a family. They envision the other benefits that having children will bring into their lives.

The word 'dream' has other meanings. It is used to describe events that happen in the subconscious, most often during sleep. A dream could also be a reverie—a "day-dream" or trance. Whenever a dream occurs, it happens in the subconscious mind.

The focus of this book hones on the dreams that people conceive in their active state of consciousness. I use the term 'sleep dream' to describe a dream captured in a subconscious state of mind. At times sleep dreams could be a stimulus for casting a vision of the future in real life. You could take the idea from your sleep dream and conceive it as a dream in your state of active consciousness.

When someone dreams, s/he takes time to envision a future s/he desires. This element of the future is a vital part of the dream process. In addition, there is an anticipation aspect to dreams, especially since, most of the time; they signal to the dreamer a favourable and desirable position. Another important element of dreams is that they could be so big and unimaginable that realizing them will be a great accomplishment to the owner of the dream. Pursuing dreams stretches you as an individual and realizing them makes you fulfilled.

DREAMS IN THE FULFILLMENT OF HUMAN NEEDS

Dreams are our attempt to fulfill our human needs and they emerge from our human longings. They constitute an essential part of our day to day living. In fact, it has been bluntly stated that he who does not dream, is dead while they are living.

Our needs as human beings are varied. Maslow is a great pioneer in humanistic psychology. He studied and described a hierarchy of human needs (3). Such studies point to the fact that if our needs are met, we are happy and our existence is fortified. If our needs are not met, we crave different ways of meeting them.

If our need of belonging and love is not met, we feel insecure. If our need of worth is not met, we feel inferior. We feel inadequate if our need for competence is not met. When our need for purpose in our lives is not met, we feel insignificant. Safety and esteem are other major categories on the list of Maslow's characterization of our human needs.

Thus, to fulfill our needs, we, as human beings, envision an ideal future where those needs are met. We dream about a better future in different facets of our lives. We have dreams that could be a vision of a place where we would like to be, or some position we would like to hold. Our dreams could also be an envisioning of some material possession we would love to have or some experience we would love to go through at a certain point in the future.

In many cases, our human needs are met as our dreams are realized and this ultimately leads to a fulfilling life in general.

In the chapters that follow, you will read about men and women who pioneered great projects and led significant lives because they had a need or saw a need in the lives of the community in which they lived. Those needs became a passion for them and they wholeheartedly sought ways of meeting them. Meeting those needs became a purpose in their lives and they fervently lived that purpose.

DIFFERENT CATEGORIES OF DREAMS

Dreams come in various categories. Your vision of the future encompasses various aspects of your life.

- Relationship dream
- Family dream
- Career dream
- Business dream

- Education dream
- Personal development dream
- Financial dream
- Spiritual dream
- Leisure/fun dream
- Sports dream
- Health dream
- Fitness dream
- Public service dream
- Legacy dream

Many dreams fall into more than one category. For instance you may want to start a business to achieve financial independence. That kind of dream is both business and financially related. You may desire to go on a missionary trip, thereby fulfilling a legacy dream that you inherited from your parent. That dream belongs to both a spiritual and legacy category. Whatever category your dream belongs to, the important fact is that your dream places you in a better position in some areas of your life.

In fact, fulfilling one dream may result in simultaneous fulfillment of dreams in other facets of your life. This is because you are not compartmentalized and neither are your dreams. So fulfilling a dream in one area tends to spill forth into other areas of your life.

In my research for this book, I found an amazing example of the dreams that people have in today's society. I have put them into the categories described above.

Table 2.1 Examples of different categories of dreams

Relationship dream	• Marry after 50 • Find new love after a traumatic divorce • Re-marry after a long interval after the loss (death) of the first spouse
Career dream	• Change careers from office administrator to animal welfare counsellor • Become a movie star
Education dream	• Finish bachelors degree in education • Study for a MBA
Financial dream	• Save enough for retirement • Pay off student loan • Work because I like to, not because I have to • Invest in real estate
Health dream	• Get on top of menopausal symptoms • Keep blood pressure within normal range
Public service dream/ Community service	• Join the Peace Corps • Create a scholarship fund for less privileged children • Teach inner city kids to play soccer
Family dream	• Adopt two children from Asia • Get pregnant
Business dream	• Own a home-based business • Launch a successful real estate business
Personal development dream	• Learn Japanese • Write a song • Get organized • Overcome fear of change • Have a regular sleep schedule

Spiritual dream	• Go on a mission trip to Indonesia • Get closer to God
Sports dream	• Go skydiving • Play sports on a particular team
Fitness dream	• Loose 30 lbs • Gain weight • Build strong muscles
Legacy dream	• Write autobiography of father • Set up a foundation in memory of spouse

Maybe you were able to relate to one or more of the dreams on the list. Perhaps, you have some unique dreams that are different from those above. Whatever your dreams are and to which category they belong does not really matter. What matters most is that fulfilling a dream could enrich your life. It could make your life more significant.

What are the stages involved in moving a dream from an idea to actually realizing it?

THE STAGES OF A DREAM PREGNANCY

You conceive a new dream as an idea that comes to you through various means. The stimulus for conceiving new dream ideas could be based on your human needs as discussed above. On the other hand, the conception could be as a result of an inspiration you received from other sources.

The new idea or dream conception tends to keep circulating in your thoughts. It tends to be your waking thoughts and the thing that dominates your mind whenever you are alone or away from daily activities. The idea becomes more real as you ponder it or imagine what your life would become if that dream was achieved. You have become pregnant with a new dream!

An essential part of moving forward is to set a specific time to see that dream becoming a reality. This is always important since that specific date becomes your estimated date of delivery (EDD). Similarly, this date is the one at which a pregnant woman expects to deliver her child. Without an EDD, it is difficult to make your goals time-specific. An example of a conceived dream is going to Hawaii on vacation. When you decide which year and month you desire to realize this dream, you are setting your EDD. That EDD will make your planning more realistic.

Once you have set your EDD, you can then plan the action steps and smaller goals to take to make that due date realistic. You are ready to engender your conceived idea as you transform your thoughts into action. Your dream begins to grow as you actually carry out those specific goals and actions. The more action steps you take, the nearer you will be to your realistic date of delivery.

While you take even more action steps, your dream moves from the first to the second stages of growth. It progresses from the first to the second trimester. At this stage, you begin to stretch yourself even more to ensure you have done all that is necessary to get closer to the delivery date. This will eventually move your dream to the third trimester of growth and pre-delivery. With adequate planning, you will have carried out all of the necessary action steps that will result in your dream delivery to occur on its due date.

In essence, your dream growth is similar to the growth of a baby during its gestation period.

• THE LENS OF THE DREAMS' MIDWIFE •

In real life, dream growth does not always follow straightforward patterns. Many a time, you face periods of no activity at all during the pursuit of your dreams. These are period of interruptions to your goals.

INTERRUPTIONS

Interruption is the act of delaying or breaking the continuity of an action or event. It is a hold-up in the course of actions. To interrupt is to hinder or stop the action or discourse of (someone) by breaking the chain of events. When there is an interruption, there is a break in the continuity of actions or events.

Therefore, when a dream is interrupted, there is an obstacle to overcome, or delay to circumvent. You have put pursuit of your dream on hold—perhaps indefinitely. The expected date of delivery of your dream is put off until a later time and your original plan may even go back to the drawing board.

How much farther your EDD will be pushed back, will be determined by the length of the interruption. This temporary cessation and period of inactivity will remain for as long as you interrupt your action steps on the path of attaining your goals in the pursuit of your dream.

INTERRUPTED DREAMS AND SPONTANEOUS ABORTIONS

Interrupted dreams, delayed goals and action steps are common events in the pursuit of a dream. In some ways, interrupted dreams could be compared to miscarriages in pregnancy. When a pregnant woman experiences spontaneous abortion of the baby, her dream of having a baby is put on hold. In many cases, the woman can revive that dream after a period of time. She can revitalize that dream and get pregnant again. She can put an end to the period of interruption and move forward again in the pursuit of her goals.

However, in some other cases, the expectant woman who experienced a miscarriage may not be able to put an end to the period of interruption or delay of her dream. If for any reasons, the woman is not able to get pregnant again, then she may not be able to revive her dream of having a baby. The interruption or hold-up she experienced in the first attempt of her dream then becomes a permanent end to the dream.

Thus, the events and course of action taken by the woman after that spontaneous abortion will determine whether the interruption will put a permanent end to that dream, delay or hold-up.

In a similar manner, you could experience an interruption or hold-up when you are pursuing your dream. However, that delay or break in the continuity does not have to be permanent. Your course of action after the period of interruption will determine whether or not that dream could be realized at a later date.

But what are the types of interruptions that you could face in the pursuit of your dreams?

DIFFERENT TYPES OF INTERRUPTIONS

As mentioned earlier, visions are your perception of an ideal future and pursuing a dream is like going on a pregnancy journey. You face challenges, meet different people and face possible distractions. You are often able to overcome some of the challenges you face easily by drawing up on your existing resources. However, because of the risks that are sometimes involved, the resources you need may not be available to you. This quickly erects an obstacle in your journey towards the delivery of your dream. It could be one of the reasons for putting the dream on hold. Such obstacles that seem insurmountable at the time you interrupted your dream are varied. Here are a number of causes of interruptions:

- Lack of financial resources
- Major life transitions e.g. divorce, death, relocation, motherhood or becoming parents, retirement, job loss
- Health-related issues such as a stroke or debilitating accident
- Inhibition by a key player in your life
- Political reasons, natural disasters such as war or hurricane
- Social and cultural norms defining what you are or are not allowed doing
- Your mindset—lack of clarity in what you really want in life. You might be too busy pursuing other things and have no time to pursue that particular dream.

These are general causes of interruption of dreams. Your dream could face any one or more of these factors during the course of your journey toward its fulfillment. In fact, there could be multiple interruptions strewn about in the path of your journey. It is noteworthy that your mindset could be the cause of your interruption. Chapter 6 gives a more in-depth analysis of the various psychological aspects associated with your mind-set.

How do these causes of interruption relate to the different categories of dreams that are mentioned earlier in this chapter?

A dream in each category could face any of the different causes of interruption. For example, interruption of a relationship dream could be caused by lack of financial resources, divorce, political situations such as war or even by your psychology. A leisure dream, such as going on a skydiving trip, may be interrupted by a health-related issue such as a recently diagnosed eye disease. Such a leisure dream could also be interrupted if you do not have enough financial resources. This lack of finances may be due to the fact that you are too busy pursuing too many other things which are taking a significant bite out of your budget. Therefore, your dream is vulnerable to a number of different interruptions.

LENGTH OF INTERRUPTION

Since the EDD is a critical factor in the pursuit of dreams, it is also essential to consider the length of interruption periods. Just as the causes of interruption are varied, the length of the delay period cannot be predicted. The interesting fact is that the length of the hold-up is not dependent on how close you are, or felt you were, to the delivery point before the interruption. Interruptions close to the delivery point can be very challenging. Chapter 9 describes how you can overcome these hurdles successfully.

At whichever point the interruptions occur on your dream journey, you do not have to make such hold-up a permanent end of the dream. A dream can be revived after periods of interruption if you put your heart and mind into it. This book is aimed at helping you to revive such interrupted dreams. Chapter 5 is devoted to breathing new life into such dreams.

• THE LENS OF THE DREAMS' MIDWIFE •

VIEWING THE CYCLE OF A DREAM IN CHILDBIRTH IMAGERY

Captured through the lens of the dreams' midwife, the following diagram illustrates the cycle of dream gestation.

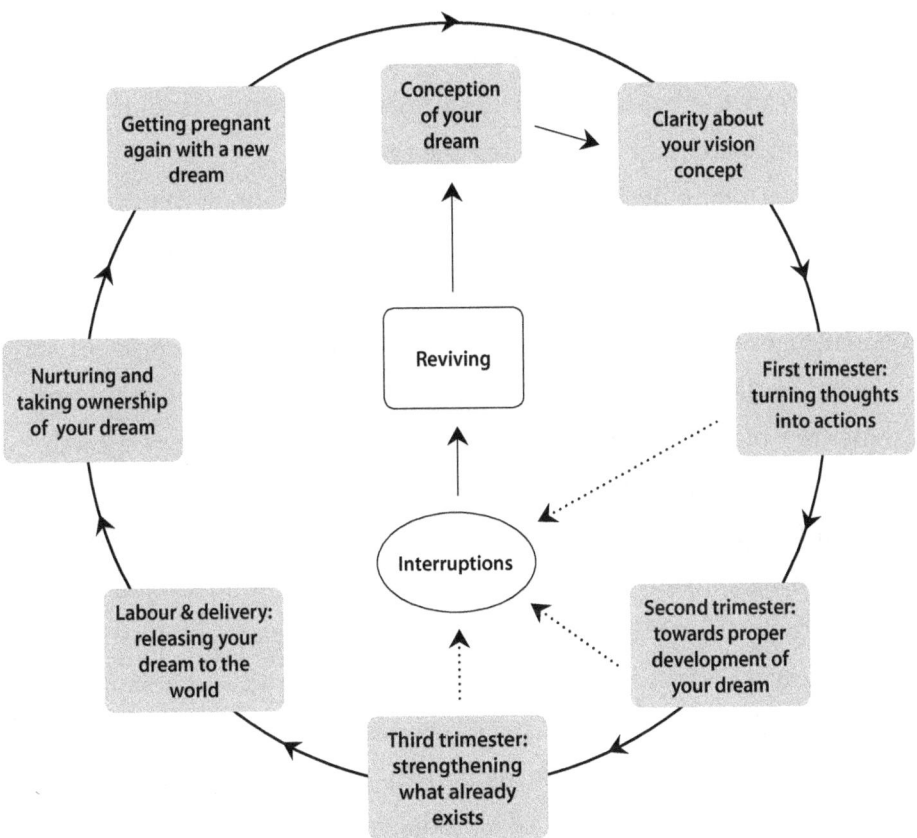

Figure 2.1 Dream gestation cycle in childbirth imagery

The cycle illustrates the various stages of your dream gestation. It highlights the fact that there could be many interruptions on your journey towards achievement of your dream. It shows that an interruption is not only a one-time event. It could happen at any of the points of transition from one phase to another. It could happen at any phase of the pursuit of your dream.

However, the crucial point is that no matter where the interruption occurred, the dream can be revived. The diagram shows that the dream can be cycled from interruption to a point of reviving. After reviving, your dream can be resumed at a relevant stage. The process of reviving will help you clarify where to resume the cycle.

This is a simplified diagram to illustrate the essentials of the dream cycle. In the remaining chapters of this book, I expand on the journey towards dream achievement. Drawing some insights from the challenges of pregnancy and childbirth, we will discuss the stages of dream gestation from conception to delivery. I also offer practical tips in order of ensuring that your dream survives each stage of growth, moves on to the next stage and is ultimately delivered.

In Chapters 3 to 6, we will discuss the essentials steps involved in reviving a dream and having clarity as to what is it that you really want to do about your deserted dream in your present circumstances. The next set of chapters (7 to 9) deals with the process of rebuilding; that of taking new actions steps towards the goals of your revived dream until you eventually bring it forth. The final set of chapters (10 to13) deals with the process of reproducing your dream achievement; multiplying the number of dreams you achieve and finally becoming an all-round dream achiever.

You will also find in the following chapters, examples of other contemporary men and women who fit well into the category of 'dream achievers'. They had different categories of dreams—career, spiritual, financial and others. They also faced different types of

THE LENS OF THE DREAMS' MIDWIFE

interruptions on their journeys towards realizing their dreams. Some had their interruptions at early stages of their dream while others had theirs close to the delivery point. But they all revived their dreams after the delay and realized them in the end.

Before I launch into the dream stages and the illustrative stories, it is important that you first take a look at your personal dream achievement history. This is an essential starting point on your journey to discovering your strength to deliver.

CHAPTER 3

Strength at Various Levels

An upfront review of your dreams fulfillment history

In Chapter 2, we discussed the various factors that could cause interruptions in the pursuit of your dream. Those factors could be within or outside your control. Whatever the reasons for the hold-up, the interruption of your dream imparts some changes in you as a person. You could have lost some strength and unconsciously developed a new understanding of your dream and life in general, or perhaps view your dream in a different light.

The focus of this chapter is a personal review of your dream achievement history. As a prelude to the exercises involved in this review, I am going to elaborate on the use of the word 'strength' in terms of realizing your goals.

IT TAKES MORE THAN PHYSICAL STRENGTH TO DELIVER A DREAM

In many circles, the word 'strength' normally brings up thoughts of physical ability for exertion; the ability to exert a force against a resistance. Such thoughts and the perceptions that male strength is superior to that of females were at the basis of the opinions held in the aeronautic industry in the early days. This was before the employment of women pilots became the norm.

Captain Meryl Getline worked with commercial airlines for many years before retiring while working for United Airlines. She is one of the first women airline captains to have launched into the career. In her book entitled *The World at My Feet*, (1) she recounts some of her unique experiences in a field dominated by men.

I had the unique privilege of interviewing Captain Meryl Getline (2) on the issue of the strength it took her to deliver her dream. Her career goal was that of becoming a woman airline pilot in the days when the social norms were not in favour of it.

She recalled that in the early days of having women employed as airline captains, people were not sure that women were *capable* of piloting an aircraft adequately. The opinion was that women were not 'strong enough' to lift such massive equipment as an airplane that carries so much weight in terms of the passengers and their luggage.

However, the perception was based on the wrong premise, since even a man of extraordinary strength could not be expected to "lift" an airplane off the ground. Physicists have proven the point long ago. The strength of the pilot has nothing to do with the lifting power required to take an aircraft off the ground. It's not about the strength

• STRENGTH AT VARIOUS LEVELS •

of the operator; it's about the power exerted by the engine of an aircraft at the time of take-off.

Captain Getline mentioned that the airline authorities actually designed tests to assess the capability of women to do this seemingly enormous task. The public had to be convinced that women did possess the physical strength to fly an airplane.

In Meryl's case, passing the assessment was just one of the challenges she had to overcome to become one of the woman pioneers in the aeronautic industry. It took more than physical strength to deliver her dream in the cultural confines of the time. However, with determination and persistence, Meryl overcame the many obstacles in her path and gave birth to her dream.

Just as in flying aircrafts, physical strength is only one of the 'strengths' needed to pursue goals. What then are the specifications for the other types of strengths required in the pursuit of your goals?

THE DIFFERENT KINDS OF STRENGTH REQUIRED TO DELIVER YOUR DREAM

The word 'strength' is used in various circles and industries. The different uses fall under one of the following categories:
- Physical
- Emotional
- Intellectual
- Intrinsic

PHYSICAL STRENGTH

Physical strength is the ability of a person to exert force on physical objects using muscular power. Various daily activities require different amounts of physical strength. Physical strength is the hallmark of the sports and fitness industry. When people undergo strength training, their aim is to increase their physical strength.

Physical strength also deals with the power of resisting an attack, e.g. conflict between persons or groups such as a military attack. It deals with the capacity for exertion or endurance.

You definitely need some level of physical strength to carry out action steps towards realization of your goals. The amount of physical strength you need depends on the goal you wish to attain. A leisure dream that requires mountain climbing will call for more physical strength than the personal development goal of playing the guitar.

EMOTIONAL STRENGTH

Emotional strength has to do with the feeling you get due to the range of emotions generated by the results of your actions or those of others in your vicinity. Emotions generated in an environment where you feel love, acceptance, sense of belonging or purpose tends to result in feelings of strength. Emotions generated by attitudes of hatred, rejection and lack of purpose, on the other hand, could sap your energy.

Emotional strength is exemplified by Dr. Martin Luther King Jr., the martyred Black American leader who fought against social injustice. In his book entitled *'Strength to Love'* (3), King advocates that if people acquired the emotional strength to love, social injustice could be conquered and his dream fulfilled. King believed that by reaching inside ourselves and tapping into the transcendental moral ethic of love, the societal evils of our times could be overcome.

This illustration by one of the greatest dreamers of our contemporary times shows that emotional strength is relevant in terms of realization of our goals.

INTELLECTUAL STRENGTH

Intellectual strength deals with the capacity to carry out a function or the faculty to do something. It involves brain power, logic, reasoning and human resources. For instance, an engineering firm could have the strength to work on ten big projects concurrently.

In politics, a party leader has the knowledge and the understanding to lead the government in the right direction.

Intellectual strength may also involve force as measured in numbers such as effective numbers of any body or organization. Thus, in terms of the number of supporters, a political party may have the strength to win an election.

Intellectual strength comes into play in the realization of many goals and dreams. Nevertheless, a faculty for logical thinking is required to plan your goals and organize your action steps towards realization of your dream.

INTRINSIC STRENGTH

Intrinsic strength defines the framework within which you live as a person. It deals with factors that are innate or inherited from your environment. It is a strong attribute or inherent asset. Otherwise referred to as talents, this kind of strength can also be developed and enhanced when you recognize them and put them to use towards your life's purpose. Someone may have the innate gift for languages and therefore could assimilate, master many more languages than most people could. Another individual may have athletic talents that prove a strong asset when s/he enters a competition. Many goals and dreams in life are weaved around such above-average abilities. Intrinsic strength is thus very relevant when it comes to your ability to carry out action steps towards the accomplishment or delivery of your dream.

THE 'STRENGTH' TO DELIVER A DREAM

All of the examples cited above attest to the fact that the realization of a dream requires a combination of different kinds of strength. Just as in the case of Retired Captain Getline's strength to deliver her dream, delivering your dream may bring into play a mix of physical, emotional, intellectual and intrinsic strengths. The constituents of the mix of the different types of strengths will vary from one dream to another. However, whatever the type of ingredients you have in your mix, your aim is to acquire the strength to deliver.

This quest for the strength to deliver also encompasses the goals of many organizations, industries and people in different walks of life. In fact, people, products or services that claim to have the leading edge in their industry, attest to their strength in delivery.

Fitness industries label their strength training equipment has having the strength to deliver. Engineering companies claim to have the strength to deliver projects on time. Financial institutions declare that they have the strength to deliver products and services for their varying customer's needs. Political parties say they have the strength to deliver a good government for the people. Press releases state that newly hired executives have the strength to deliver change that will profit global companies.

As described in Chapter 2, the birthing process requires a lot of stamina. Birth coaching classes are aimed at equipping mothers with the physical strength to deliver. Expectant mothers also need more than physical strength to realize their childbirth goals. They need to be emotionally fit to overcome the challenges of pregnancy. Thus, pregnant women, like other dreamers, employ different types of strength in their 'strength to deliver' mix.

STRENGTH IS GAINED WHEN A DREAM IS FULFILLED

In Chapter 2, I mentioned the role of dreams in the fulfillment of our human needs. When your dream is fulfilled, your human need is met and this results in a range of emotions. The type of emotions generated depends on the type of needs required in fulfilling the dream.

If your relationship dream is fulfilled, you will feel loved and secure. If you achieve your career or business dream, you will feel capable and competent. If you were able to realize a legacy or public service dream, you will feel worthy and experience self-esteem. If your financial dream is fulfilled, you will feel satisfied and content. Realizing a personal development dream makes you feel competent and worthy. If your leisure dream goals are achieved, you may feel rejuvenated or experience joy and self-satisfaction.

Thus, fulfillment of dreams could make you feel capable, significant, competent, satisfied, worthy, accepted or secure. All of these positive emotions reinforce your emotional strength. If you have the majority of your needs on various dimensions met, you will even feel stronger and energized. This emotional strength is translated into physical strength for your normal day to day activities. You are ready to live out your life with more acuity than someone who is struggling to get their dreams fulfilled.

STRENGTH IS LOST WHEN A DREAM IS NOT REALIZED

On the other hand, if your dream resulted in a disaster, or something that you never want to touch again, obviously your needs were not met. If your dream was interrupted by factors beyond your control, you will also lack the feeling of fulfillment. Your unmet needs may make you feel inferior, incapable, insignificant, inadequate, unloved and insecure.

All of these negative emotions result in the draining of your emotional strength. You feel weak emotionally and this often translates into physical weakness.

If you have a significant number of your dreams being interrupted or resulting in disasters, you may have a feeling of being burnt out or sapped of strength.

The loss or gain of emotional strength that accompanies the incompletion or the non-realization of dreams is a critical factor in your zest for life in general.

Having established the strength factor, let us take a glimpse at your perception of your levels of strength at various times.

MEASURING YOUR STRENGTH AT VARIOUS LEVELS

The following is a self-examination exercise. Take some time to reflect on your past life.

• **STRENGTH AT VARIOUS LEVELS** •

Strength at high levels

On which occasions did you feel very strong? What happened at those times? In the space below, write down as many as you can remember. Include those in your childhood as well.

_____
_____
_____
_____
_____

Strength at low levels

On which occasions did you feel weak? When did you feel as if you had lost all your strength? What happened at those times? In the space below, write down as many as you can remember. Include those in your childhood as well.

_____
_____
_____
_____
_____

Take a look at your first and second lists. Can you see a pattern? Is there any connection in the levels of your strength and the periods of your achievements?

_____
_____
_____
_____
_____
_____

With this background of your varying levels of strengths, let us perform a review of your history of dream achievement.

CREATING YOUR LIFELINE

This next exercise calls for some introspection. It will help you take a deep look inside your past life. To some extent it will also help you cast a vision of your future. It may be emotionally moving for you to perform. However, it will be worth your time and attention. In fact, it could be a life-changing exercise for you.

The exercise is in two parts. The first part deals with key goals and dreams you have achieved in the past and those you propose to achieve in the future. The second part involves dreams that you worked on in the past and which resulted in disasters or were interrupted or abandoned.

• **STRENGTH AT VARIOUS LEVELS** •

PART ONE—ACHIEVED DREAMS AND REALIZED GOALS

In the space below you will find a horizontal line. This is your lifeline. The line represents the length of your time on earth—the period when you are living. The line will be used to mark the key events in your past life. You will also be able to insert expected key events in your future.

---

a. On the far left end of the line, insert a dot and label it with your date of birth.
b. Estimate how long you might live. Somewhere near the far right hand side of the line, insert another dot to represent the projected number of years you will be alive. Do not place this dot at the end of the line, but somewhere in between the middle and the far right. This is so that you can insert some goals that go beyond your life span. Take extra time to complete this step.
c. Next, insert a point on the line that represents today's date. Label it.
d. Now, you need to fill in the section between your date of birth and today's date. Insert at appropriate points to the left of today's date, labels representing key goals and dreams you have realized in the past. These are events such as:
- graduation from school
- purchase of your cars
- marriage
- buying your home

- job and career appointments
- birth of your children.

The events you listed in the 'Strength at high levels' exercise above may help you identify the key events for this part.

Make sure you do not rush this exercise.

e. Now, you can insert your projected goals for the future in the right hand section of the line. This is the section to the right of today's date. Insert key goals and dreams that you desire to realize in the future as points on this section. Include goals that you expect to go beyond your life span.

Figure 3.1 shows an example of a life line

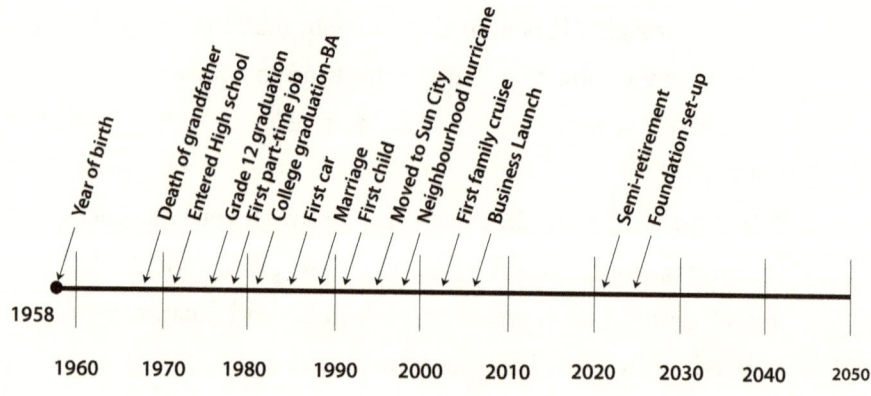

Figure 3.1 Example of a life line

• **STRENGTH AT VARIOUS LEVELS** •

PART TWO—DREAMS THAT RESULTED IN DISASTERS AND DREAMS THAT YOU ABANDONED

This second part is aimed at creating a lifeline that shows:

a. your dreams that resulted in disasters and

b. your interrupted dreams and abandoned goals.

The events you listed in the 'Strength at low levels' exercise above may help you identify the dreams and goals for this part.

Ask yourself thought-provoking questions that bring hidden truths to the surface. Ask yourself the question:

If I were to die today, what would I have regretted not having accomplished?

Use this second horizontal line to repeat the steps in Part One (a)—(e) above.

Insert the dates corresponding to:

a. when some dreams you had became disaster e.g.
- deaths of your relations
- divorce or break-up of a major relationship
- collapse of business
- theft of major possessions
- natural disasters such as hurricane and so on.

b. when some of your dreams were interrupted as in the examples below:

Examples of interrupted dreams and abandoned goals:
- You interrupted your career pursuit due to family reasons, e.g. a woman raising a family.
- You started working on a career change from a highly prestigious one to another for which you showed more talent or passion. However, you were interrupted because of an inhibiting factor imposed by a key player in your life, e.g. family member or boss.
- Your goals were interrupted due to political pressure or bureaucracy. Your country's foreign policy no longer allowed foreign instructors to teach at the university or technical institute where you were pursuing your dream to become a professional some day. Therefore, you were never able to complete that dream.
- You were drafted into national military service, went to war for a couple of years and your relationship dream was sidetracked. When you got back, you discovered that your girlfriend was married to another man. You decided not to pursue any new serious relationships and your marriage dream has remained abandoned ever since.
- Your father died at an early age and you had to take on more responsibility because you were the first child. You had to get into the workforce quickly with minimal education. You had started training towards becoming a private pilot but had to abandon it.
- Your mother re-married and then had much younger children, whom you had to baby-sit. You barely had time to do any girls' stuff. You had to give up the community classes you were taking towards becoming an interior decorator.

• **STRENGTH AT VARIOUS LEVELS** •

When used with the first lifeline you created, this second lifeline will help you identify what might be missing in your life. In the next few chapters, we will discuss the interrupted dreams and projected goals that you listed in depth.

STRENGTH LEVELS DURING INTERRUPTIONS

In Chapter 2, we discussed the subject of interruption periods during the pursuit of your dreams. We saw that there could be one or more delay periods in your journey towards realization of your goals. These periods of interruption could happen at any phase of your journey and the time interval cannot always be predicted.

Earlier in this chapter, I pointed out that your emotional strength levels correspond to your moments of dream achievements or the lack thereof. The question is what happens during periods of interruption of your dream? What are your emotional strength levels when you face delays or you put your dream on hold due to circumstances beyond your control? Do those delays represent periods of low or high levels of strength?

MULTIPLE HOLD-UPS OR DELAYS

As it is possible to have many hold-ups in the course of one's dream cycle (See Figure 2.1), it is noteworthy to consider the issue of strength levels against a background of multiple interruptions.

Consider a dream that you conceived and started pursuing. Assume you worked on it up to the 'first trimester' stage and you had to abandon it. Then after a period of six months, you revived it and started taking action steps again towards realizing the dream. You were all enthusiastic that you would realize the dream the second time around. However, that did not happen. Instead, you faced another interruption which lasted a full year. Thus, the dream went on a cycle of 're-starting and interrupting' a number of times. How were your strength levels during those periods of interruption?

MY STORY—A DAD'S DREAM FOR ONE OF HIS CHILDREN

As I mentioned in Chapter 1, the launching of my coaching career is part of a bigger legacy dream. This legacy dream was passed on to me by my father who was a practicing pharmacist for a significant part of his life. Like most fathers in my cultural background, my dad dreamt that his children would take up careers in medicine, pharmacy, and law. My dad's dream was realized over time. I started off my career in pharmacy and so did one of my siblings. Two of my other siblings took up careers in medicine and law.

However, my dad also had this other related dream that one of his children would become a minister of the gospel. I grew up in a family of eight children, so there was a reasonable probability that at least one of us would take up this career. As it turned out, neither I nor any of my siblings became a career minister of the gospel.

My dad's dream was not getting fulfilled. Somehow, at a later stage of his life, he re-conceived this dream. He re-organized the dream into a new context. My dad went through a change of career and became a minister of the gospel. He sold the chain of pharmacies (drug marts) that he had and went through seminary training to become an ordained minister. So my dad's dream was realized in some way. However, the fulfillment was not achieved in the context he had originally envisioned. It was not one of his children that fulfilled it. It turned out that it was a partial fulfillment. The best was yet to come.

• STRENGTH AT VARIOUS LEVELS •

Somehow, around the period of my dad's passing, this legacy dream of a career path in ministry was passed on to me. (I recounted my career change experience in my book—*Stay Sane Through Change* (4). As I received new revelations of my life's purpose, I literally ran with the idea. I took hold of a vision of an ideal future in this new career path. And I set out to pursue the dream wholeheartedly. The vision became a legacy dream for me.

When you are 'captured' by a legacy dream, you will feel a void in your life until you fulfill it. You might accomplish so many other great feats, but you will feel incomplete until you realize that particular dream. My legacy dream became one that defines me and the purpose of my life.

MULTIPLE INTERRUPTIONS OF MY LEGACY DREAM

Fulfilling my dad's legacy dream became a pivot around which other events in my life revolved. I had great enthusiasm about the goals towards fulfilling the dream right from the time I conceived it. That moment of conception of the dream was a point of 'high-level strength' for me.

Recounting how I felt at that time, it seemed alright to predict a nearby estimated date of delivery for the dream. However, I faced multiple interruptions during my pursuit of this vital dream. Those interruptions have been both challenging and interesting. I have had multiple periods of high-level strength as well as low-level strength.

The first set of goals and action steps that I took towards fulfilling my legacy dream was to attend seminary. It seemed the obvious pathway towards changing careers into that of a minister of the gospel. More importantly, I was convinced that it was the way for me to go. The decision was a major one, considering my background career and previous job experiences in pharmacy and biotechnology. Determined and geared up by new revelations of my ideal future, I overcame many obstacles in my path towards launching myself into the training. Though challenging, the period of my seminary attendance was mostly that of 'high-level strength' for me. Going for what I was meant to do in life was very liberating, which came with positive emotional strength.

I faced my first major interruption a year after I started attending seminary. I had been enjoying the release process and was all set to complete the second year of my two-year course towards a Master of Arts in Christian Education. However, I received a new revelation that had an urgency attached to it. I was to go back to my local church and volunteer my services to the leadership. Alongside this new vision, there were other factors that made it extremely difficult for me to continue the seminary course.

Therefore, I took on action steps towards the new goal of working at my local church. I understood that this was a re-organization of goals towards fulfilling my legacy dream. Even though my first major goal of seminary training was interrupted, I had not abandoned my legacy dream. That perception helped me to take on the new assignment with eagerness and zeal.

RE-LAUNCHING DREAM IN A NEW CONTEXT

In a period of two years after I started the volunteer local church work, I had different interruptions, re-organization of goals and new re-launching. In this period, I launched a business with a slogan—'pursuing excellence for women in transition'. I perceived that my life's experiences and my mission could be directed towards women who were stuck through periods of life-changing transitions. Launching that organization was a period of 'high-level strength' for me.

However, not too long after that, I got zapped again to go back to my local church. I had to put the work with women through that business on hold. Back at my local church, I got involved in a missions' project. My experiences while working on the project and during the actual missionary trip was another liberating experience for me. It was a moment of high-level strength. My legacy dream was being fulfilled in some way as I went through this various moments of liberation. It was not the way I had set out to accomplish it. However, the interruptions, re-starting and re-organization were moving me forward as I realized more goals.

After the missions' project, I received a new revelation about a book-writing project. As I mentioned in Chapter 1, I received a new vision in a sleep dream that pointed to the fact that I was pregnant with a book project that was due to be birthed. The idea was great, but there was another element to it that I did not quite understand. I was to co-author the book with the senior pastor of my local church. As with many of the turning points in the pursuit of my legacy dream, there was an urgency attached to the vision. Once again I decided to re-organize my goals towards fulfilling my legacy dream. And again I took on the new goal project and pursued it wholeheartedly.

RE-ORGANIZED GOALS IN A NEW CONTEXT OF MY DREAM

Working with new zeal and renewed strength, I realized the goal of launching a new book co-authored with my senior pastor nine months after I received the new vision. During the period of release of the book, *Stay Sane Through Change*, I experienced high-level strength. A few months prior to the book release, I launched a new business with my co-author F. David Webster. I saw that as a new vehicle for reaching out not just to women, but also to men and women who needed a message of hope. Dave and I set out to equip people to use times of change as stepping stones to greater fulfillment in life. Armed with our new book, we reached out to our target audience through many avenues. Dave and I were featured on many radio talk-shows and had some local engagements sharing our message.

NEW CONTEXT, NEW TRAINING

Expanding our concept further, we launched out to reach more specific target audiences such as career changers and those who have experienced divorce. Then I saw more light. I decided to get certification towards life coaching. I realized my legacy dream was taking on many new shapes as I progressed along the way. My experiences with multiple re-launching and re-organizations of my goals had given me a better perspective. I understood that my journey was as important as my ultimate goal.

Working towards the goal of launching a career in life-coaching stirred up a significant amount of reactions. In Chapter 1, I discussed how the wheel of events in my life was hopelessly clogged. So, I went through another period of interruption, re-organization, re-launching and moving forward. During this period of hold-up, I received more insights and revelation. I finished my coaching course, sat for the exam and even took some business building courses.

• **STRENGTH AT VARIOUS LEVELS** •

NEW CONTEXT, NEW MESSAGE, NEW REVELATION

Since the unclogging of the wheel of events in my life, I have received new strength to deliver my legacy dream. This book is a testimony to that fact. I have dedicated *Strength to Deliver* to the memory of my father. I believe it is a significant action step for receiving his legacy in its fullness. It is an essential step towards propagating the legacy which my dream entails.

In addition, I have great passion for my role as the dreams' midwife, helping men and women to birth their dreams. I love to work in particular with those who have deserted their interrupted dreams.

My legacy dream is being fulfilled and I definitely understand my vision more than I did when I started. Fulfillment of my legacy dream is an ongoing process. This book is a stepping stone towards the accomplishment of more dreams that will carry on into the future for many generations to come.

GAINING FROM INTERRUPTIONS

It is evident from the story of the pursuit of my legacy dream that one can face a number of interruptions on the journey to realization of their dreams. It is also noteworthy that predicting the length of interruption periods is difficult, especially when they are caused by factors that you cannot control.

Since these periods of delay are common factors in the pursuit of dreams, what use can you make of them? How can you gain from periods of interruptions of your dream?

To reshape a period of interruption into a positive experience, you need to have an open mind to analyzing it. Here are some positive things that could be achieved through periods of interruption of your dream:

1. Gaining of personal growth. With the right attitude, you can develop maturity over the period of interruption of your dream.
2. Enjoyment of greater motivation for higher goals if you channel your anger positively.
3. Opening of doors for innovation and new ways of doing things.
4. Creation of an attitude of resilience—the ability to stay on top of challenges or set-backs.
5. Stimulus for challenging the status quo and stretching your imagination.
6. Access to even greater opportunities. You are equipped for greater achievements in the future.

On a personal note, I have come to enjoy the process towards the fulfillment of my legacy dream. I cherish the stopping points on the journey. I have acquired new strength to deliver along the way. I value my personal growth and many other unplanned dreams that I accomplish during the journey.

THE WOMB OF SUCCESS

Another way to view periods of interruption is to consider them as the time when your success is growing in the womb. That concept is the theme of a book by a group of ministers called *Failure—the Womb of Success* (5). A group of twenty men and women related experiences of interruptions or failures, which ultimately turned out to be the starting point for successes in their lives. Your period of delay or hold-up of your dream can also be viewed as the womb of your future success.

• STRENGTH AT VARIOUS LEVELS •

YOU HAVE A UNIQUE HISTORY OF DREAM ACHIEVEMENT

Before I move on to the next chapter, I encourage you to take a close look at the lifeline you created earlier in this chapter. No matter what that lifeline holds, one thing is certain; you have a unique mix of achieved dreams, disasters and interrupted dreams.

The component of your mix of achieved dreams, disasters and interrupted dreams is particular to you. Your mix is not the same as anybody else's. That makes you unique. No one else has your history of dream achievement. Others may have histories that are similar, but it can never be identical to yours.

This particular fact of uniqueness makes you special. And that is a strong point to hold onto as you consider what to do with those vital dreams that are in the abandoned state. This is the focus of the next chapter.

CHAPTER 4

Strength and Purpose

Why it is important to re-consider your interrupted dreams

In Chapter 3, I discussed an exercise in introspection whereby you went through your life history, listing the dreams you have had thus far. The dreams on your list were placed in three categories: (a) accomplished dreams, (b) dreams that were utter disasters and can no longer be touched and (c) dreams on which you were still working, but abandoned along the journey towards their achievement. Those abandoned dreams in category (c) are the focus of the rest of this book.

In this chapter, I discuss how you can take a new look at those dreams that you started working on but never got to realize. It will be important to pass those abandoned dreams through a grid and weigh your options. Now, let's see how you could review those deserted dreams through the lens of your strengths and life's purpose.

The analysis should help you clarify which of those abandoned dreams you may want to bring up from the dungeon back into the light. It will help you identify which deserted dreams to revive, re-conceive, grow and ultimately bring forth.

STRENGTH AND PURPOSE: A TWO-WAY STREET

In the world of dreams fulfillment, strength and purpose are part of a two-way street. They are two ingredients that work hand-in-hand to make life meaningful. The life of someone who has a great amount of strength with no understanding of his life's purpose can amount to wasted time, effort or even lead to destruction. On the other hand, someone who knows his/her purpose in life but has no strength to fulfill it, makes no headway.

A MAN OF GREAT PHYSICAL STRENGTH

The biblical story of Samson (1), a man of great strength, illustrates the importance of channelling strength into meaningful purpose. Samson was a man dedicated to God from birth. He was born into a special class of people called Nazirites, which means 'set apart for God'. In fact, a special mission was assigned to him right at the announcement of his conception. He was to begin to deliver his nation, Israel, from the hands of their long-standing captors, the Philistines.

Samson was destined to be a great man. This high endowment came with huge responsibility; he was not to cut the long locks of hair off his head. Samson spent the early part of his life performing great feats such as killing large numbers of his nation's opponents with the jawbone of a donkey. He had enormous physical strength. However, for a significant part of his life, Samson used his strengths for practical jokes and getting out of disasters that resulted from his careless attitude.

• **STRENGTH AND PURPOSE** •

Over time, he became even more careless with his Nazirite responsibilities of being wholly dedicated to God. Despite his parents' advice, he dated and got married to a woman from a non-Hebrew tribe. That was against his unique dedication as a Nazirite. This big mistake led on to many others in the life of Samson. Gradually, his strength was directed to less meaningful conquests. His life became out of balance. He was not in sync with who he really was.

A LIFE NOT LIVED TO ITS MAXIMUM POTENTIAL

Samson's wrong choices eventually led to his being captured by the Philistines. He had been lured to revealing the secret source of his strength. His enemies took advantage of that knowledge and took him as their prisoner. Ironically, his captors were the very people he was supposed to capture in the course of his life's mission. The destined captor became the captive.

At the end of his life, Samson was given an unusual privilege. He manifested even greater strength than he ever did before. Samson killed many more people on the occasion of his death than all through his life combined. And it was recorded that he did begin to rescue Israel from the hands of the Philistines. At his death, Samson actually began to do what he was destined to do for 20 years while he was a judge with Nazirite strength!

So, on the long run, Samson is remembered mostly by his defecting from his Nazirite responsibilities and for being lured by a foreigner to reveal the source of his strength. Samson had the potential to strengthen his nation, annihilate the ever-present enemies of his people and even return his nation to the true worship of God. But that just remained a potential, which never became a full accomplishment.

In essence, Samson was a man of great strength but found wanting when it came to the issue of purpose. That isolation of purpose from the manifestation of his strengths resulted in a life not lived to its maximum potential.

LET YOUR STRENGTH WORK IN SYNC WITH YOUR PURPOSE

Thus, it is important to have strength and a sense of purpose working together as you re-consider your interrupted dream. Ask yourself the questions:

What does the interrupted dream play in my life's purpose? How can my strengths help me towards realizing this dream, which plays a significant role in my life's purpose?

To answer this you do need to know both parts to the question.

What are your strengths?

What is your life's purpose?

To live a life of purpose you have to live your strengths. You have to know your strengths and maximize them by channelling them into the avenue of your life's purpose.

FINDING YOUR STRENGTHS

In Chapter 3, I discussed the different types of strengths you need in the pursuit of your dream. Also in the same chapter, during your upfront review exercises, you were able to identify moments of your life when you felt strong and moments when you felt weak.

Psychologists have designed various assessment tools to help you decipher your areas of strength. Such assessments are based on your emotional, intellectual and intrinsic strengths. There are many of

• STRENGTH AND PURPOSE •

these available on the market place and a comprehensive review is outside the scope of this book. Some of the strength assessment tools focus on personality while others focus on aptitudes and interests. One such tool, based on the Mayerson's Foundation work, is called the *Signature Strengths* assessment. It was designed by a team headed by Martin Seligman, a professor at the University of Pennsylvania. This VIA Strengths Survey is available through the website www.authentichappiness.org.

The survey is based on 24 strengths in the areas of courage, wisdom and knowledge, humanity and love, justice, temperance, spirituality. The website provides users with a feedback after they complete the assessment.

The Clifton Strengthsfinder® is another useful assessment tool for discovering your strengths. Designed by a group at the Gallup organization, the Clifton Strengthsfinder® access can be obtained through one of their publications (2).

Other tools for discovering your strengths include the Strong Inventory Assessment®, which is based on aptitudes and interests and the Myers—Briggs®, which is well known for personality testing. Both of these are available online through various web-based assessment sites.

To make the best of these strength assessment tools, you may need to work with a professional such as a life coach. During the process of discovery, such a professional can help you find which of these tools is best suited to your particular circumstance. They can also help you translate the results into meaningful interpretations and work on developing those strengths further.

EMBRACING YOUR STRENGTHS

As you discover your strengths, you need to embrace them and work towards maximizing them. You need to focus on your strengths to help you towards giving birth to your interrupted dream. Acknowledge your weaknesses, but do not focus on them. Do not let them deter you from this new attempt at realizing your goals. As you maximize your strengths, you will be able to achieve your purpose. You will find out that living your strength is purposeful living.

But you do need to know that purpose first.

DISCOVERING YOUR PURPOSE

Knowing your life's purpose is an essential step towards a fulfilled life. Simply put, discovering your purpose is like figuring out what you want to do with the rest of your life.

Purpose is the object for which one strives or for which something exists. It is a result or an effect that is intended or desired. Purpose is also taken as a determination or a resolution.

Many times people face cataclysmic situations or life-threatening challenges. For instance, a 23 year old woman had a major car accident on her way back from a campaign trip. A 56 year old man had to go through heart surgery when he had a debilitating stroke. The list goes on. When people come out alive from such experiences, they tend to live their 'new life' with renewed vigour and a distinct sense of purpose. To such individuals and to every one of us, our life's purpose could be viewed as:

- The reason why you are alive while someone else who had a similar experience as you had is dead;

• STRENGTH AND PURPOSE •

- The reason you got a job position and someone more qualified than you did not get it;
- The reason why you are given a chance (most often a second chance) at life;
- For parents passing on legacies to their children, the children can take their life's purpose from the reason of their parents' passing and leaving the legacy behind for them to carry on.

But you do not have to wait until you are faced with life-changing situations before you can discover your life's purpose. You can discover your purpose right now.

AN EXERCISE IN FINDING YOUR LIFE'S PURPOSE

Ask yourself the following questions.

What are my aims in life? What am I striving for? What are my goals in life? What am I determined to achieve in life?

Spend five minutes in writing down some unique statements that provide answers to such questions. Then take another 10 to 15 minutes to revise the statements you have written. You may choose to combine some of your statements into several different versions of your purpose statement.

If you are having difficulty with this process, you can reflect for some time on your past life. Write down instances when you were filled with the most sense of fulfillment/accomplishment for something you had done. Those were the times you felt 'on purpose'.

Here are some sample purpose statements:

My life's purpose is to promote the well-being of my family and those entrusted to my care.

My purpose is to become an accomplished, famous violinist.

I aim to radiate God's love through serving others.

You may desire to work on writing your purpose statements in a group or with friends with whom you can gain more insight and creativity.

Now write your purpose statement below:

_____
_____
_____
_____
_____
_____
_____

There are more resources listed at the end of this chapter for discovering your purpose (3-5). You may also want to work with a life coach on life purpose discovery.

• **STRENGTH AND PURPOSE** •

THE POTENTIAL OF THE KNOWLEDGE OF YOUR STRENGTH AND PURPOSE

Discovering your life's purpose combined with knowing your strengths puts you at the door of great potential. However, unless that potential is utilized, the knowledge of who you are and what you have will amount to nothing.

Although, the construction of dams is becoming a subject of environmental controversy, the wisdom behind these great engineering structures is still fascinating. Dam construction is based on the principle of converting energy from a natural resource—a waterfall—into electricity. Engineers build dams to tap into the huge energy of water gushing down a hill at high speed. They tap into the power generated by the falling water. Then they convert this power (mechanical energy) into electrical energy. This electrical energy is supplied to homes and offices, becoming power sources for myriads of daily activities. Great wisdom! However, what happens if this energy is not tapped into? It will still be awesome scenery, but the waterfall's potential will not be maximized. The water keeps on gushing down the fall, but has no purpose. The energy which would otherwise have been useful is just 'wasted'.

Mere knowledge of your strength and purpose without tapping into them is just like an un-dammed waterfall. The potential will just be sitting there, left unused.

Therefore, the question is: what do you do once you are clear on what your life's mission is and when you know your strengths? The answer is simple and straightforward:

Go ahead and fulfill your life's purpose by living out your strengths. When you live out your purpose through your strengths, you will be in harmony with your true self. If you fail to use your strengths towards your purpose, your life will be out of balance.

Living out your strengths is purposeful living.

Here is the story of one man who did that well. It is the story of Cardinal Joseph Mezzofanti.

HOW MANY LANGUAGES CAN A PERSON SPEAK?

Cardinal Joseph Mezzofanti (6) is one of the greatest polyglots of all times. He was a man well ahead of his time. He lived in the 18th century (1774—1849) but still holds the world record for multi-language fluency. He is credited with a perfect knowledge of 38 languages and a less perfect knowledge of 30 other languages and of 50 dialects. That is one of the greatest personal development dreams ever achieved!

What is more extraordinary about Mezzofanti is the fact that he learnt all of these languages without leaving his home-country of Italy. He acquired his mastery entirely from books or through native speakers, who visited the Vatican.

Mezzofanti obviously had an unusual combination of strengths; a strength to rapidly assimilate languages and a prodigious memory. He turned this strength into a powerful purpose in his life. He started his language exploration at an early age. When he was twelve, Mezzofanti already spoke nearly ten languages. He tapped into resources of Jesuit missionaries from different lands who taught in his grade school. He learned Latin, German, Ancient Greek, Spanish and Central and South American indigenous languages. As a very bright student full of enthusiasm for learning, Joseph finished the studies for priesthood early, but could not be ordained because he was too young. Joseph spent the period in between the end of his studies and his ordination very wisely. He engaged in the study of Middle Eastern and Oriental languages. At 23, he was ordained and became the Professor of Semitic Languages at the University of Bologna. Not long after, Mezzofanti had another interruption in his career. He lost his university position because he refused to pledge allegiance to the Cisalpine Republic when that republic was formed.

This political interruption did not discourage him from his quest for learning and practicing languages. Rev. Mezzofanti became the chaplain for hospitals in Bologna during the battles of 1799 -1800 in Italy. In this position he was able to converse with wounded war victims and learn more languages. It became very clear that Mezzofanti had a unique sense of purpose.

LIVING OUT YOUR STRENGTHS IS PURPOSEFUL LIVING

Mezzofanti's strength and sense of purpose was all-encompassing during his entire career. His love of study, although very prominent, was not restricted to languages. He also devoted himself to the study of ethnology, archaeology, and astronomy. Mezzofanti also performed the duties of his holy ministry well and he was referred to as the "Confessor of foreigners".

In 1803, Cardinal Joseph regained his professorial position in Classical Languages. In 1831, he moved to the Vatican where he became the head of the Vatican Library. While in Rome, Mezzofanti dedicated much effort to learning languages from the missionaries, clerics, professors and dignitaries of the Church. In order to learn Chinese, he went to the Capodimonte College for foreign missions, in Naples.

All through his life, Mezzofanti exploited his strength of phenomenal memory to master an enormous list of languages. The level of mastery he acquired is testament to the fact that he tapped into his strength to fulfill his life's purpose.

As I discussed above, strength and purpose are like twins working together. This association is evident in the story of Joseph's life. The use of his strength was not isolated from his purpose. When Joseph had interruptions in his education and career, he employed the time wisely and learned more languages. He was thus further developing his strength. He increased his language mastery through the exposure that came as part of his normal career as a priest and a professor. On the other hand, the ability to speak so many languages helped him in his work as a priest and Head of the Vatican Library.

Cardinal Joseph Mezzofanti is one man who lived out his strengths. And that is purposeful living!

A NEW LOOK AT THE INTERRUPTION PERIOD OF YOUR DREAM

Cardinal Mezzofanti's story demonstrates that interruption periods could be viewed as periods of growth. Those periods could actually help enhance the dream delivery process when you revive it at a later date. Thus, although you did not plan for such, periods of interruptions between major action steps towards your dream fulfillment could have positioned you better for success.

It is therefore imperative to explore what happened during the period of interruption of your dream. It will serve a good purpose to take a deep look at the other events which took place and at the other goals you realized during the period when you were not working

STRENGTH AND PURPOSE

on that particular interrupted dream. Such analysis will help you recognize what has changed in you as a person since you deserted the dream. Most importantly, such an exercise will help you discover new strengths that have become apparent in you that may be relevant to your new attempt to pursue the dream.

Equally as important, you will be able to discover what route your life has taken in terms of your life's purpose since you deserted the dream. You will be able to figure out whether this route is in alignment with the life's purpose you have newly discovered. In essence, the exercise will help you position yourself better and affirm your decision to revive and ultimately deliver that interrupted dream.

Using the lifeline you created in Chapter 3, pick on the first major interrupted dream that you dumped, i.e. the one that has been inactive for the longest time.

Now take a look at the period between the time you dumped your dream and this period when you are considering reviving it.

List all other major dreams you have accomplished between those two periods. List other ways in which you have grown as a person.

List other major events that have occurred in your life during that period of interruption. These could either be events that you cherish or events that you wished never happened.

_____
_____
_____
_____
_____
_____
_____

As you look at your list, you may recognize that you have realized some other goals and dreams in the in-between period. Those dreams and goals may not be particularly related to that first major interrupted dream. However, in your process of waiting, you have grown in other respects. You have actually conceived, and delivered, some other 'unrelated' dreams and reached previously 'unplanned-for' achievements.

Maybe, you had some other disasters on the way as well. These have given you opportunities to learn and recognize vital truths about life.

Thus, your period of interruption could be regarded as growth phases of your journey towards success.

VIEWING YOUR INTERRUPTED DREAMS THROUGH SPECIAL LENSES

Now that you have recognized that the interruption period of your dream could actually be viewed as a stepping stone, let's take a closer look at those interrupted dreams. We will consider those abandoned dreams that you listed in Chapter 3.

Re-write in the space below the list of dreams you previously started working on but left unfinished.

Also write down the dreams that may be necessary to take you to a place you desire in the future.

_____
_____
_____
_____
_____

A view through the lens of your strengths

In the space below, list the strengths that you discovered in you, using the tools mentioned earlier on in this chapter.

_____
_____
_____
_____

Now take one abandoned dream at a time and ask yourself the question:

Were there any weaknesses of mine that accounted for my incompletion of the dream?

The contrary question is: what kind of strengths did I not use when I abandoned the dream? Which necessary ingredients were deficient at the time when I first attempted the dream? Write these down in the space below.

Weaknesses /deficiencies

_____
_____
_____
_____
_____

With the new or refreshed knowledge of your topmost strengths in mind, ask yourself:

If I am to revive this dream today, which of my strengths will help me accomplish this dream?

Newly recognized and/or renewed strength

_____
_____
_____
_____

Performing this exercise will help you recognize that you have what it takes to revive that dream and complete action steps towards bringing it forth. It will boost your confidence in your abilities.

A view through the lens of your purpose

This next exercise will help you check the relevancy of your abandoned dreams to your newly-discovered life's purpose.

Insert here your revised and updated version of your purpose statement.

_____

_____

_____

_____

_____

Now take a look at each of the abandoned dreams that you listed above and see whether they are in alignment with your vision of the future. Also check them against your life's purpose statement and see whether fulfilling that dream is in line or in opposition to your life's purpose. Analyze this dream in terms of where they fit in different areas of your life (i.e. relationship, financial, spiritual, career, leisure, health).

This exercise will help you put each of the abandoned dreams on a scale of relevancy in your ultimate fulfillment in life.

You will recognize that, while dreams may all seem important, some dreams are more crucial to your life's fulfillment than others.

HOW RELEVANT IS THAT ABANDONED DREAM TO YOUR LIFE PURPOSE?

It would be great if you could revive all of those interrupted dreams that fit, to some extent, into your life's purpose. However, it makes sense to prioritize which interrupted dreams to revive first.

This next exercise will help you identify which of your interrupted dreams is most important when you are considering where to spend your time and effort.

The exercise will help you discover those dreams that are intertwined with your life's purpose.

On an imaginary scale of 0 to 100, rate each of the abandoned dreams you listed above according to their relevancy towards attaining your life's purpose. If you feel the dream is very relevant, give it 100 while if it is not relevant give it a 0.

_____
_____
_____
_____
_____

INTERRUPTED DREAMS THAT ARE ENTWINED WITH YOUR LIFE PURPOSE

When a dream is intertwined with your life's purpose, leaving it in an unfulfilled state may jeopardize many other areas of your life. However, if such a crucial dream is fulfilled, it often spills its many benefits onto your life in general. This is because it often takes realizing that one essential interrupted dream is intertwined with your life's purpose to get you going. Fulfilling that one or a couple of dreams will set you on the path towards realizing more dreams and goals. It will equip you with that strength to deliver in many facets of your life.

Most often that one dream or set of dreams is the "rate-limiting" one dream. That one dream—if it stays unaccomplished, many other things in your life will tend to stay in limbo.

In high school chemistry, I learnt about the rules of chemical reactions. I learnt that there is one critical step when it comes to product yield when two or more substances are combined. That step is called the "rate–limiting-step" of a chemical reaction. This is the step that determines the overall rate at which the end products are formed from the reaction of two or more starting chemicals. If that rate-limiting-step is hindered, the reaction will not go forward.

Your crucial dream is that rate-limiting one, the one on which most other important things in your life hang upon.

Stop that dream, and your life will seem to go round in circles without going anywhere or reaching any destination.

COUNTING THE COST

Now focus on those dreams that are high on your relevancy scale towards attaining your life's purpose. It does not matter whether they achieve a score of 100 or less. The fact is you have recognized that they are relevant to some extent.

Take time to count the cost of the two major options you have; to revive or to leave it in the abandoned state. Ask yourself:

What is it costing me to leave this dream in the abandoned state?

Based on your new knowledge of your strengths and life's purpose, ask yourself:

What will it cost me to revive this dream?

When you have identified the relevancy of that interrupted dream to your life's purpose, you will be more confident to revive it. You will come to terms with the fact that you have the right to conceive this dream again.

You will have cogent reasons for reviving it and working on it. You will be certain that it will be worth your effort and investment in time and money. The process will be affirming as regards your next step towards reviving the dream.

AN INTERRUPTED LEGACY DREAM ENRICHED WITH ACHIEVEMENTS

The plot of the 2004 movie, *The Terminal* produced by Steven Spielberg (7) provides an interesting illustration as to how the interruption period of a dream could serve as a period of major growth in an individual. It demonstrates that many other disparate but complimentary dreams could be achieved during the interruption of a major dream.

Viktor Navorski (a character played by Tom Hanks) had a legacy dream that was passed onto him by his father. It was a passion-driven dream. Viktor's dad had found a photograph of a Jazz band with 57 Jazz artists in a magazine. His passion had driven him to seek out all the 57 artists to collect their various autographs. That dream, that took 40 years to see it to completion, was almost complete when Viktor's dad passed away. In his dying wish, the father had made Viktor promise that he would collect the only one remaining autograph and add it to the collection. The last jazz artist lived in New York and it was only a matter of a trip and the dream would be accomplished.

Thus, Viktor traveled all the way from his fictional country of Krakozhia to New York City to fulfill his father's legacy dream. Viktor took this mission seriously being the dying wish of his dad.

COMPLICATIONS OF DREAM DELIVERY

Just before delivery, Viktor encountered numerous difficulties that almost prevented him from giving birth to this dream.

On arrival at New York airport, Viktor met with troubles due to bureaucratic policies. He was denied entry into the United States. Viktor discovered that during his flight, his country's government had been overthrown by rebels, making his passport invalid. This was a major problem, which left Viktor stranded. He could neither enter the United States nor go back to his home country. He had to take up residence at the terminal where he made new friends.

After nine months, the political situation in Viktor's country was resolved and his passport became valid. After another obstacle, Viktor was able to take a cab into New York City to visit the jazz artist and collect his autograph. Thus Viktor's dream was ultimately realized.

AN INTERRUPTION PERIOD ENRICHED WITH MANY ACHIEVEMENTS

Viktor had to wait for about 9 additional months at the terminal doing things that he never planned on doing originally. Nevertheless, he achieved many unplanned dreams in the process of waiting. He took employment at some construction company thereby getting American work experience on his resume (even though it was at the airport).

He had some romance; a bit of relationship dream that was not quite completed. He made new friends, spoke English more fluently than when he first arrived (personal development achievement). He even helped some unknown person to overcome immigration bureaucracy because he had studied the rules in his spare time.

All in all, the mini-dreams he conceived and delivered in the process of waiting made him grow into a better person and fulfilled his life in general. Viktor became more fulfilled than he would have been had he not been interrupted; if he just went straight to get his document signed and returned to his home town. In the end, he not only accomplished his dad's legacy dream, but he reached his own goals and delivered some of his dreams too. He did not just collect an autograph, but he 'lived' the American life and experienced it. He added new strengths and experience to his life on his journey towards the dream's fulfillment.

STRENGTH AND PURPOSE—AN ENIGMA OF A COMBINATION

In the remaining chapters of this book, there are various examples of people who demonstrated that they recognized their life's purpose and discovered their strengths. And using the combination of the newly discovered strength and renewed purpose, they revived some dreams they had previously abandoned. Some of these people had health-related interruptions while others were inhibited due to lack of financial resources. Some were delayed by a key player in their life while others had to interrupt their dreams for family reasons.

However, whatever the reason for the initial abandonment, these people picked up their dreams after they received a fresh stimulus to re-start. During the period of interruptions they had acquired new strengths as they worked on other related or un-related dreams. They were given renewed purpose that served as motivation to revive their interrupted dream when they received appropriate stimuli.

Some of these men and women had discovered their strengths in the area of courage, wisdom and knowledge, humanity and love. Some discovered that their strengths lie in areas of spirituality, justice or temperance. These newly displayed or recognized strengths were very handy when they re-launched their interrupted dreams.

The interruption periods also gave the people a renewed sense of purpose. Some actually discovered the purpose of their lives during the period of deserting their dream. That combination of renewed strength and sense of purpose became important in gathering momentum along the way. The stories of such men are illustrated alongside other concepts for reviving, conceiving 'protruding', bringing forth your dream.

MOVING FORWARD WITH YOUR RENEWED STRENGTH AND OPTIMIZED SENSE OF PURPOSE

Just as Viktor in that movie, you need to recognize that your interruption has actually done some good in your life. You need to view that positive aspect of it and hold firmly on to it.

You have been able to identify that you are not the same as you were when your dream was interrupted. You need to move on with that new confidence gained from your awareness of the fact that your interruption period has made you stronger. It has helped you grow in some areas. You need to hold on tightly to that combination of strength and newly affirmed purpose. You need to hold on to your new awareness as you gather strength to revive that interrupted dream and launch new actions towards its fulfillment.

The next chapter deals with what it takes to breathe new life into the dream.

SPECIAL NOTE

You may use the services of a life coach for help in discovering your life purpose.

To locate a life coach that is your match visit the International Coach Federation website at www.icf.org

CHAPTER 5

Strength to Revive

Breathing new life into your interrupted dreams

In the previous chapter, I discussed why it is important to take a fresh look at the dreams you previously abandoned. One of the major reasons mentioned is the fact that one or a few of your unaccomplished, abandoned dreams may be the crux to your life's purpose. One interrupted dream that you have dumped may be the reason you are always searching for something that seems missing in your life.

Having discussed the premises for re-considering those interrupted dreams, the question arises as to which steps to take to recall those dreams. What do you need to do to restore that vital dream from an inactive state to an active goal worth pursuing? How do you bring your deserted dream from the cool back burner to the hot front burner? This chapter will address these questions.

WHAT DOES IT MEAN TO REVIVE?

Reviving is a process of breathing new life into something or someone. It is a process of restoration, renewal, restarting or revitalization.

In medical circles, the process of reviving or breathing new life into a person is called resuscitation. Resuscitation is the act of restoration of life or consciousness to one who appears to be dead or who is dying. Later on in this chapter, I explain how resuscitation is a useful analogy in the breathing of new life into an interrupted or abandoned dream.

Reviving may also be a form of resurgence, which is a continuance after interruption or a restoration to use, acceptance. Reviving is also a form of resurrection which is the act of returning to life, the act of bringing back to practice, notice or use. In a more obscure term, reviving is revivification, the act of recalling; the state of being recalled to life.

Therefore, when I talk about reviving an interrupted dream, essentially, I mean bringing back that dream from a dormant state, a state of inactivity to an active one. When you revive an interrupted dream, you resume taking action steps towards its fulfillment after you re-clarify your concept by re-conceiving it.

REVIVING AS RESTORATION OF AN OLD DREAM

There are two aspects of reviving a dream that are equally important. The first is the ability to restore a dream that you previously started but deserted in mid-stream. For example, you started to learn to play the guitar but never quite mastered your skills enough to play meaningfully in a band setting. Now there is a major opportunity for you in your new environment that is almost perfect. However, that guitar mastery skill is essential to that position. You can choose to work towards attaining that important position by reviving your dream of mastery of guitar skills.

REVIVING AS RESTORATION OF THE CAPACITY TO DREAM

The second aspect of reviving that is also essential to your ability to perform maximally is the renewal of your *capacity* to dream, the bringing back to life of your dreaming *capability*. This type of reviving is essential if you have experienced deep grief such as a series of catastrophic events that left you overwhelmed. These events might have left you with very little zest for life. They might have left you with no hope for continuing on your life's path. In that case, the process of reviving is one of breathing new life into your 'womb' and re-activating your capacity to dream. I discuss more of this in Chapter 6.

Let us explore further how to know whether you may need to breathe new life into a dream that you previously deserted. What are the warning signs that indicate your need to do something about those dreams? How do you know you have to stop ignoring the obvious and take necessary action?

SIGNALS THAT INDICATE YOUR NEED TO REVIVE A DREAM

Here are some signs that may demonstrate that you need to dig into your past and pull out the remnants of a deserted dream:
- You are restless always searching for something that seems not be existent in the present
- You have a reduced or minimal zest for life
- When you imagine your life as a script, you feel an urgent need to rewrite some vital parts of the script. You wish you could re-play essential parts of your earlier life

- You are feeling unfulfilled in life in general. You are searching for a life of significance. The list of things you desire deep inside does not match the position you currently occupy.

HINTS FROM YOUR LIFE HISTORY

In Chapter 3, you created a life line. That lifeline could also be used in checking whether you need to pull out an old dream and start working on it. So, take some time to review that life line again in the light of any of the warning signs listed above.

But, how much effort do you really need to dig into the past and pull up that abandoned dream? How strong should you be to attempt such an escapade? How much emotional, physical and intellectual strength do you need to revive that vital abandoned dream?

HOW MUCH STRENGTH DO YOU NEED TO REVIVE YOUR INTERRUPTED DREAM?

As creatures of habit, we human beings tend to resist any form of change. Thoughts of changing for something entirely new are daunting even though changes may be exciting. Changes that require picking up something not entirely new, but previously attempted and abandoned may even be more overwhelming. The scarier the task, the more strength required to pull it off.

However, the re-assuring thought is that in many cases, once we are able to overcome that initial inertia and revive that dream, the effort required to keep it going may often be less.

That first critical step is the rate-determining step; the one that will tell you whether the dream will stay forever abandoned or will see the light of day in a new fashion.

The level of strength required to pull out an old dream from the dump, 'dust it' and put it back into active mode depends upon a number of factors.

FACTORS GUIDING THE PROCESS OF REVIVING

(a) The stage at which dream was interrupted

Using the imagery of childbirth, you may determine whether you abandoned the dream at conception, first/second/third trimester, labour or delivery stages. In other terms, this stage of interruption is based on the percentage or fraction of the total number of goals you have accomplished towards delivering the overall dream. How many more goals are required for you to score a 100% for the dream to be accomplished?

It seems a logical conclusion that if all of the other factors were irrelevant, reviving a dream that was abandoned at pre-labour stage is expected to be easier than one interrupted at the first trimester. Consider a dream of finishing college interrupted after the 1st year as compared to when it was interrupted at the last semester before graduation. More motivation may be required for the first individual to pick up that dream than for the second individual. However, there are other relevant factors that influence your motivation to revive an abandoned dream.

(b) The relevance of that interrupted dream to the fulfillment of the individual's life's purpose

The importance of completing that dream in the fulfillment of your life's purpose (as illustrated in Chapter 4) is a very important factor in finding the motivation to pick up that dream from its abandoned state.

(c) The length of time that the dream was left in an abandoned state

In the world of plants, resuscitating a water-dependent plant that is almost withered requires much more effort than one that was abandoned (and did not receive water) just for a few days. In terms of dreams, a common day example is a dream of fitness. If the last time you worked on your goal for a healthy weight was 20 years ago, it may require more motivation to get back on track compared to someone who dropped that dream a year ago.

That being said, always remember that it is never too late to pursue a dream that you truly desire. The story of Jenny Wood-Allen the woman who completed the London Marathon race at age 87 is a testimony to this fact (See Chapter 10).

(d) Your present environment

In Chapter 2, I mentioned how your mindset could be the cause of interruption of your dream. It is possible that you abandoned a dream in mid-stream because your mindset was 'opposed' to the realization of your goals. Your frame of mind during the pursuit of the goal may have resulted in your inability to fulfill the dream. Therefore, a major factor in the reviving of a dream is your present mindset and environment. What has changed since you abandoned the dream? Are you in a better frame of mind than you were when you dropped it? Are your circumstances better? Is your environment more conducive towards working on the goals? The answers to these vital questions determine the ease with which you can revive your interrupted dream.

THE 'ABC' OF RESUSCITATION

As I mentioned above, reviving can be in form of resuscitation, breathing new life into someone who has lost consciousness, has fainted or has 'passed out'. The following is a very simplified account of what resuscitation entails.

The goal of resuscitation is to ensure that both the breathing and the blood flow functions of the body are maintained. The standard procedure for resuscitation is termed 'ABC': airway, breathing, and circulation (1).

A. Airway

The first essential of resuscitation is to ensure that the person's airway is clear. This is achieved by pulling the jaw forward or, through skilled assistance, by using a special tube passed into the windpipe.

B. Breathing

Once the airway is clear, the patient may begin to breathe spontaneously. If this does not happen, it may be necessary to force air into the lungs by mouth-to-mouth resuscitation or by using a special medical apparatus.

C. Circulation: cardiac massage

The follow-up step after the airway is clear and normal breathing has resumed is the maintenance of blood flow to the tissues. If this does not happen spontaneously, urgent cardiac massage is applied to the patient. This involves compressing the heart against the spine by rhythmic pushes on the breast bone.

THE ABC OF REVIVING AN INTERRUPTED DREAM

These principles of airway, breathing and cardiac massage may be applied in synonymous terms to the process of reviving an interrupted dream.

A. AIRWAY CONTROL
De-clutter your life

When the paramedic works on a choking victim, the first goal is to remove the object that blocks the airway. They have to remove the obstruction in the airflow. It will be difficult for the individual to breathe if the airway is blocked. Oxygen cylinders available for resuscitating the victim will be of no use if it cannot get through the airway to the lungs.

This seemingly obvious analogy also applies to the process of reviving an interrupted dream. Before you can breathe new life into your abandoned dream, you have to remove the obstruction from the windpipe. You need to take out those old items that are obstructing your ability to breathe. You need to remove some physical stuff from your environment that is preventing you from having mental and physical space for new things. You need to de-clutter your environment—your living space and your working areas. Sort the items into the categories: 'to stay', 'to trash'; and 'to be handed to someone else'.

Remove the things you do not need. Sort them into those that should be dumped and those that should be given to someone else. If your interrupted dream is in the area of physical fitness, you may need to de-clutter your refrigerator and pantry. Empty your fridge from these items that may prevent you from attaining weight control or maintenance. Dump the old, leave the necessary ones that will help you in resuming the pursuit of your fitness dream.

It is not only your environment that you need to de-clutter. You need to remove the clutter from your mental space, from your mind, from your thinking. This is especially important if you abandoned your dream because of a life-changing event or emotional trauma. You need to remove the emotional debris from the past, which are obstructing your ability to think rationally. One important way to do this is to forgive the past. I will elaborate on this particular subject later in this chapter.

You also need to de-clutter your relationships. At times this may involve leaving a particular environment for another.

You need to de-clutter your intellectual space—that area that deals with your ability to perform. One way to do this effectively is through stocktaking which I explain later in this chapter.

To get new hope for living and starting afresh on your interrupted dream, you have to dump the old clutter and breathe new life to the remaining solid (non-clutter) items.

B. BREATHING
Channel your anger into the positive route.

Remember to breathe properly. Channel that anger into the right direction. Have you ever wondered how much effort is required to breathe when you are angry as compared to normal conditions?

It could be that you are angry because you did not meet your expectations in terms of fulfilling that dream the first time around. You can channel that anger into a positive path to accomplish great things in your new circumstances.

Anger is a strong emotion of discontentment caused by some type of grievances that the person either sees as *real or perceives* as real (2). It may be a perceived disrespectful treatment in terms of needs, beliefs, thoughts and feelings. It may be a perceived threat to a lifestyle to which you are accustomed.

The long term effects of frequent or chronic anger include hypertension (high blood pressure), aggravated heart disease, damaged or blocked arteries, depressed immune system resulting in increased susceptibility to infection.

But anger does not have to lead to bad side-effects. It could be used in a positive way. Dr. Lyle Becourtney, a New York Licensed Psychologist and certified anger management professional, has this to say about channelling anger properly.

> *"Although uncontrolled anger can be quite costly, when channelled properly anger can also be very positive. Among other things, anger can motivate us to work harder to accomplish our goals"* (3).

Fuelled by anger and the desire to prove others wrong, many people have pursued new and higher level goals. They channelled their feelings of displeasure into a positive path.

Many great activists in history were angry and could not refrain from talking about wrongs in the society. They were not passive about things that really bothered them such as injustice. They got angry with the way things were. Then they set out to do something to correct those wrongs. A typical example is Martin Luther King's popular opposition of discrimination against black. His dream was a great public legacy dream fuelled by anger against wrong.

Let your anger motivate you to do something positive to make things better. You can accomplish great things when you channel your anger about your previously unaccomplished goals into a positive path.

C. CIRCULATION
Massage your memory cells

Massage your memory cells by taking refreshers. Let the blood flow to the grey cells so that your memory is re-focusing properly. Be ready for action by taking refreshers. Rebuild confidence in yourself.

Without those refreshers, a simple or great mistake may happen during the new course of action towards fulfillment of the dream. Such a mistake may end up in the revived dream heading towards another disaster. That is what happened in the case of a great king in Biblical times who attempted to revive an interrupted dream without enough refreshers.

INADEQUATE STIMULATION OF MEMORY CELLS THAT BACKFIRED

In a striking Biblical story, a popular king—David—worked hard to reinstate peace and order to counteract the tumultuous condition prevalent when he officially ascended the throne (4). King David felt that amongst other issues, it was paramount to restore his people to true worship of the God of Israel. He had the dream of reviving the practice of consulting with God for guidance through the Ark. The Ark at that time held the tabernacle where the priests of the land consulted with God. It was indeed a very desirable dream for a great leader like David. Although it is what God expects from the leaders of His people, the practice of seeking such guidance had been abandoned for a long time; during the reign of David's predecessor to the throne. In fact, it had not been practiced for about 20 years. A major action plan towards fulfilling this dream was to bring the Ark to Jerusalem, the city of David. Before then the Ark resided in a city of Israel's opponents who had captured it during a battle.

Therefore, to carry out this reviving of true worship, David executed a plan that did not work out well. One of the young men who carried the Ark was struck dead because he failed to follow the rules required for this sacred act. It led to a major disaster in the reviving of a dream, which ultimately resulted into further devastation and misery.

What went wrong? The fact is that reviving a tradition that had not been practiced for 20 years could be an enormous task when it involves not just one person, but a whole group of people.

Firstly, in 20 years, a new generation of people emerged after the practice was initially abandoned. This group of young people may not have been fully aware or cognisant of the rules. This new generation needed to be taught the rules prior to undergoing the revival of the practice.

Secondly, the generation existing 20 years prior to the time of the new reviving, who knew the rules initially, might have forgotten them. The rules had not been put into use for a long time. This segment of the population also needed to refresh their memory of the rules.

The first attempt at reviving something that has been abandoned for a long time may seldom work, especially if the rules are not followed thoroughly. Therefore, it is essential to re-acquaint yourself with the rules of the game. Knowledge is power.

If your dream involves leading a group to accomplishing a difficult task, let all the team members familiarize themselves with the rules of the game. Teach them the rules. This is relevant, especially when it comes to reviving an old practice.

If you hold the starring role in the execution of your dream, it is still as important for you to take a refresher course on how to play the game involved in the execution of that particular dream.

When you have the intellectual expertise, then you can be more confident to move forward effectively. You will be able to receive necessary stimuli to help you revive and re-conceive the dream, and take intelligent actions towards its realization.

COMMON HINDRANCES TO RESTORATION OF YOUR DREAM

Here are some common hindrances that prevent you from pursuing the quest to revive your interrupted dreams:

- Mindset, e.g., a fear of failure or negative perception of your ability
- Inability to forgive the past
- Lack of clarity on what went wrong the first time you attempted achieving the goals towards the dream
- Not having control over your own resources
- Focusing on your weaknesses
- Lack of confidence
- Thinking it is too late
- An environment that is not conducive.

A SECOND CHANCE AT LIFE

Beck Weathers is a Dallas-based physician. In 1996, at age 49, he had great dreams for his life. He was then a 'middle-aged' man looking ahead to the other half of his life, full of hope for more exciting experiences.

In search of thrilling adventures, in 1996, Weathers joined a team of nine other climbers to explore the Everest, the tallest Mountain in the world (5). That experience turned out to be a life-changing one for Weathers. In fact, it was a 'life-impacting' one in which he was 'left for dead' for almost 18 hours. However, he 'resurrected' himself and managed to show up at camp to the astonishment of his team members!

Invigorating adventures had been part of Beck's life style for a long time. In his thirties, he discovered that mountain climbing helped him to cope with depression, something that had hung over his life since his college days. However, over the years, this seemingly effective, self-prescribed therapy became more of an obsession. In rapid succession, Beck had attacked the mountains McKinley, Elbrus, Aconcagua and Kilimanjaro.

This devotion to mountain-climbing had made Beck self-absorbed, neglecting his wife and children. In fact, he was estranged from his wife when he went for the near-death experience of climbing Mount Everest. His indiscriminate thirst for adventure had led to a deep drop in his attention to his family relationship goals. He had robbed Peter to pay Paul.

Dr. Weathers had left no stone unturned in ensuring that his Everest Climb would be an exciting experience. He had paid $65,000 for the expedition. Being near sighted, in his previous climbs, he had worn lenses and contacts, which quickly became brittle and foggy under these extreme icy conditions. This created vision problems for him during the climb. To avoid this in his Everest climb, Beck had undergone an eye operation called radial keratotomy about eighteen months prior to the Everest climb.

With this kind of preparation and positive mindset, Beck was set to go. Unknown to him, this eye operation provoked the worst vision he ever had while climbing mountains. In fact, at high altitude, the altered eyes could not work properly, making him practically blind.

Beck's Everest expedition was plagued by a number of unfortunate events. On May 10, 1996, Everest was visited by one of the most devastating storms on record. Temperatures went down to 60 below zero and the wind whipped through the cliffs at 70 miles per hour. These conditions led to the death of eight members of the expedition team including four men in Weather's team.

Beck was separated from his group because of the difficulties he experienced due to his eye condition. Being practically blind, whipped by the wind, and freezing, he fell.

LEFT FOR DEAD

Beck's body was fully covered with ice, including his face, when his team members came by. They checked him, and finding no indication that he was still breathing, left him for dead. Beck heard their conversation and their decision to leave him, but was unable to respond. Lying down in the snow for almost 14 hours, Weathers thought of his family back in Texas, pondering how he had neglected them. He realized he could die in moments and never see them again.

Somehow he decided to fight back. Working slowly to move his fingers and then his arms, he eventually rose to his feet. Blind, he started shuffling in the direction he thought his camp was located. He then wandered close enough to the camp and his team-mates saw him. Blinded, gloveless, caked with ice, he looked like a 'dead man walking'.

A helicopter rescue team finally came to his aid. Interestingly enough, it was his wife's persistence that led to the organization of his rescue.

How did Weathers get the strength to 'resurrect' himself? He recalls that some force within him rejected death at the last moment and then guided him into the camp and the shaky start towards his return to life. His will to live was further strengthened by thoughts of his family.

STOCKTAKING DURING PAINFUL RECOVERY

Beck's rescue was only the first step to his new life. He had lost both hands, and his face was so badly frozen that it looked barely human. He had to undergo extensive facial reconstruction and go through a period of painful recovery.

During his recovery period, Beck did a lot of introspection. He looked inside himself. He spent some time doing an inventory of his past life. In his moments of deep search, Beck 'found himself' again. In his book, *Left for Dead*, (6)

Beck stated: *"For the first time in my life, I'm comfortable with my own skin. I searched all over the world for that would fulfill me, and all along it was in my own backyard."*

REVIVING A FAMILY RELATIONSHIP DREAM

Weathers also had to face the issue of his relationship with his family. He recognized that, apart from his physical wounds, there were some emotional wounds to heal as well. He re-conceived a vision of what he would like the future to be for him and his family. He had been given a second chance at life and he was determined to make the best use of the special privilege.

Beck's experience had given him a fresh perspective on life. Beck says, *"I no longer seek to define myself externally, through goals and achievements and material possessions"* (5).

The experience was a powerful stimulus, a zapping one that made Beck come to acknowledge his shortcomings in his family relationship. It caused him to revive that dream of loving relationships with his wife and two children. He breathed new life into what really matters the most—his relationship with his loved ones. Beck Weathers acquired new strength to work on nurturing those relationships, which he had neglected for far too long. He acquired renewed 'strength to deliver' his newly recognized mission.

MORE TIPS FOR REVIVING AND REVITALIZING YOUR DREAM

Here are some more tips to ensure you have success in breathing new life into your interrupted dreams.

1. Take your position in the driver's seat

It is important to acknowledge that, in this new attempt towards realizing your dream, you are the driver of the vehicle. If there are any other fellows involved, they will need to occupy the passenger seats or else they are out. No other person can drive this new attempt for you.

This attitude may require a shift in your mindset. A process of reviving your dream may require a rebirth on your part. This re-birth may be a fundamental change in your beliefs. It may require a change in the way you view yourself or your capabilities. Ask yourself the question: What is hindering me from attaining my own objective?

For instance if your dream is to achieve total independence, you may require a mindset shift to actually believing you are the one in control—the one to make all of the decisions. Assume that you have no fairy godmother. Recognize that you are the master of your own circumstances.

2. Break the fear cycle

Fear of the unknown or fear of failure is a real cause for the inability to move forward. You can break the cycle of inertia by taking a few steps in the right direction. Just try something different, but something that will set you off in your action path. The motivation will gradually come as you slowly acquire speed and renewed focus. You will soon realize that your initial "baby steps" were "giant moves" in the conquest of your inner fears. Once you have gained some momentum, the motivation will be self-sustaining as you focus on your strengths and purpose rather than your unfounded fears.

3. Forgive the past

Forgive those who played different roles in the interruption or the disasters that prevented you from accomplishing your dream the first time around. An attitude of resentment towards those who erected the barriers towards fulfilling your dream originally may not help you seize new opportunities and using them to your advantage. With an eye turned away, you may not be able to see clearly the new opportunities as they present themselves; you will not be able to grab them and use them to your advantage in your new circumstances.

The need to forgive the past is important not only in terms of reviving an interrupted dream, but it is essential throughout the various stages of dream conception, growth and delivery.

4. Perform more stocktaking exercises

In Chapter 3, I discussed an initial review of your achieved goals, interrupted dreams and dreams that turned out to be utter disasters. That was like a run-through of major events in your life. Further stocktaking is necessary as you narrow down the focus on your interrupted dreams. Take a critical look at what happened with those dreams.

Write down the various action steps that you took towards fulfillment of that dream before it was interrupted.
- Which steps worked? Which steps did not work? What lessons can you learn from both sets of experiences?
- Which action steps should you list as a possible option in the light of your current position and ability?
- Which action steps should you dump all together, i.e. don't try this again this time around?

In addition, analyze the factors made you interrupt the dream. Then, affirm your purpose for picking up this dream afresh as discussed in Chapter 4. Affirm that the factors which made you dump the dream previously will not be in your way as you re-start. Then say a mental 'good-bye' to that attempt at the dream.

It is time to start afresh. With your short list of possible ways to re-attempt it, you will be ready to re-conceive the dream.

5. Take ownership of all your resources

Now that you have listed possible ways in which to tackle those actions and goals anew, you need to know which resources you have at your disposal. It is essential to have a mental control over all of your resources so you can use them at the required time and in the appropriate fashion. Taking ownership over your resources implies taking responsibility for their management. When you are in total ownership of all of your resources, then you are in the position to allocate them to whichever area you need to get your dream fulfilled.

6. Capitalize on your strengths

In Chapter 4, I discussed the importance of focusing on your strength in terms of fulfilling your life's purpose. In the reviving of your interrupted dreams, it is vital to capitalize on your strengths, and not on your weaknesses.

Know your limitations, but do not let them draw you back. Rather, use your strengths in circumventing the set backs that may otherwise be inhibitive through your weaknesses.

7. Launch out with renewed purpose

Just as Dr. Beck Weathers did when he was given a second chance at life after his Everest disaster, you should launch out with renewed purpose as you revive your interrupted dream. It is essential to have your life's purpose, which you wrote in Chapter 4, in front of you as you restart. That renewed purpose will help keep you on track as you face new obstacles or hindrances that may present themselves in this second attempt at working on your dream. Keep your life's purpose constantly in mind.

8. Regain confidence in your self by looking at your past successes

Earlier in this chapter, I discussed massaging your memory cells by taking refresher courses in the area of that interrupted dream. These refreshers will help you regain confidence in your abilities.

One other way to boost your confidence is taking a look at your past successes. As discussed in Chapter 3, you have done some great feats in the past. The fact that this particular interrupted dream did not reach delivery does not mean you are incapable of achieving it. No, you are quite capable. Recall your past successes and move forward with confidence in your capacity.

9. Use your new circumstance as an advantage

View your new circumstances as an advantage and not as a draw back in the reviving of your interrupted dream. Think of it in this way. You are older than when you first abandoned the dream. And that means you have more experience. You have more reasoning power, more vantage power now than you had in that period when you dumped the dream.

Your interrupted dreams can be revived as you learn to forgive the past, remove old obstacles, have a mindset that makes you see and grab new opportunities in your new circumstances. The purpose of reviving a dream is so you can re-conceive it in your present circumstances. This new conception leads on to new growth of the dream and its ultimate delivery. In the next chapter, I discuss what it takes to re-conceive your previously interrupted dream.

CHAPTER 6

Strength to Conceive
Re-starting naturally or by means of assistance

After reviving your interrupted dream, an essential step to moving forward is re-conceiving the dream. You need to acquire the strength to conceive or re-conceive your desired goals and envision of an ideal future.

Strength to conceive implies having the capacity to imagine and have an idea about something. It indicates the ability to get pregnant or engender something, the capacity to go from "inception" to "conception"—to make a start. There is also the element of apprehension or understanding to the capability of conception. Whether you are conceiving a dream for the first time or re-conceiving it after a period of interruption, you need to be able to capture by reason or imagination what the concept of your dream means. Thus, having the strength to conceive or re-conceive involves the process of imagination, envisioning and clarifying—clarity of mind.

ABILITY TO CONCEIVE NATURALLY

In medical terms, the ability to get pregnant is naturally present in a significant percentage of the human population. For these naturally fertile people, conceiving a baby seems to be a given. However, having the capacity to get pregnant is only the beginning. Not everyone who has that capacity may actually get pregnant when they want to.

Doctors, midwives and other professionals offer lots of advice on the issue of getting pregnant. In terms of re-conceiving your dream, you also need to take action. One of such is a mindset check. The question is how do you overcome the initial hurdle to getting pregnant?

OVERCOMING THE INITIAL BARRIER TO RE-CONCEIVE YOUR DREAM

In Chapter 2, I mentioned various factors playing a role in the interruption of your dream. One of these factors is your mindset or attitude.

For you to get excited about taking up a previously interrupted dream, you need to get rid of negative thinking and overcome any fears about your vision of an ideal future. A woman who desires to get pregnant removes any birth control device she has previously inserted. She stops taking birth control pills. After reviving your dream, you have to get rid of any attitude that puts you in the position of not being able to conceive ideas. You need to keep up with those reviving tips such as taking your position in the driver's seat (See Chapter 5). In addition you need to be in a positive frame of mind.

Do not be confined by cultural beliefs or tradition. Do not allow someone else's perception of what a possible result of the dream might be. Recognize that many novel ideas first meet with resistance. Human beings naturally like to resist change. Hold on firmly to your beliefs about the ideal future that your dream conception portrays.

When the fear of the unknown is high on your mind, reflect on your past successes to rebuild your confidence. Overcome the fear of failure by recognizing that dreaming big always involves an element of risk. However, failures can be turned into stepping stones for the ultimate delivery of your dream. Take your inspiration from positive stories of people who achieved even the wildest dreams conceived. Take on the affirmations of your renewed strength and sense of purpose discussed in Chapter 4. Continue positive affirmations of your strength to bring forth an ideal future in terms of your revived dream. Re-assure yourself many times over of the fact that *"you can do it."*

The process of maintaining a positive frame of mind is a continuous one. If you need help in dealing with issues that make it difficult to be in a positive frame of mind, consider working with a life coach.

RESOLVING IDENTITY ISSUES IN CONCEPTION

For demolishing the barriers of negative mindset in re-conceiving your dream, you may need to resolve identity issues. This is especially important if your dream was previously interrupted due to inhibition created by a key player in your life such as a boss or a family member. If you faced interruption of a relationship dream due to divorce or break-up, you might have gone through a period of low self-esteem. For you to conceive a new dream or re-conceive such an interrupted one, you have to recognize that you are worthy. Participate in activities that will build your self-esteem and raise your perception of the fact that you are capable and worthy.

To pull down the barriers to re-conceiving your dream, it is also essential to heal the past. I discussed this in Chapter 5. You may have conceived again but you lost it because of spontaneous abortion. Do not allow your hurt from past interruptions of your dream prevent you from this new re-conception. You have said a mental goodbye to the past. Hold on to your view of the ideal future. Move forward confidently towards that vision as you re-conceive it.

Recognizing your unique identity as an individual is also important even if your dream has not faced any previous interruption. When you conceive the idea of an ideal future, you need to know that it is your own concept. You do not have to compare yourself with somebody else or your dream concept with someone else's. Your dream is as unique as you, the owner of the concept.

YOU HAVE THE RIGHT TO CONCEIVE ANY DREAM YOU DESIRE

The fact of the uniqueness of your identity also puts you on solid ground when it comes to the kind of dreams you conceive. Recognize that you have the right to dream big. You have the right to cast any vision you desire.

You have the right to conceive a dream that shatters an existing status quo. Do not allow someone to take away that right through brainwashing. Do not let anyone, who looks down on you and your ability, call up your "wild" concepts or hinder your progress. You have the right to cast a vision of a future that requires knocking down walls, which might stop you in your progress. You are free to let your imagination go wild. Being fully aware of your right to conceive puts you in the right frame of mind for action.

At times when couples are unable to conceive naturally it has to do with abnormalities in the structures of reproductive organs. The gynaecologist performs the checks on the man and the woman to diagnose any such anatomical defects. In some cases, surgery could be performed to correct such abnormalities and the woman/man re-gains the ability to conceive naturally. For a woman, such corrective surgery can be loosely termed reviving the womb.

In analogous terms, if you are finding it difficult to conceive your dream, you may need to perform body checks to re-gain your right to conceive naturally.

CLARIFY WHAT YOU REALLY WANT

As I mentioned above, conceiving involves a process of clarification. When you clarify your dream, you are spelling out what you really desire to see happen in your ideal future. Clarifying and visioning go hand in hand. To clarify, you need an understanding of the end result of your action steps and goals. Clarifying also involves knowing when you want to realize the dream. The process of clarifying removes any confusion about the process of working towards the dream and the outcome of such action steps. When you work on clarifying the dream concept, you will be engaging your mind into working on the goals and actions again. Clarifying is a continuous process throughout the journey of a dream. And it is an essential one from the very beginning.

If you are clarifying a previously interrupted dream, it is essential to recognize that your circumstances have changed from when you first started out, before abandoning the dream. Clarifying will help you elucidate what you really want to achieve through the dream in the light of your new circumstances. For such interrupted dreams, allow your imagination to go wild. Stretch your imagination of the concept even more than you had conceived it the first time around. Go bigger with the dream.

    Deidre's original dream was to obtain a teaching degree after a four-year study in a university. After completing her freshman year, she had her first baby. She interrupted the dream for many years as her family involvement grew. Ten years after that interruption, Deidre decided to revive her dream. With new options available, Deidre could complete one more year of schooling in a community college and obtain a teaching diploma instead of a degree. That choice would result in her getting some kind of certification towards teaching. However, that would also mean that Deidre would be lowering her original goal of obtaining a bachelor's degree. What Deidre could do in the light of her new improved circumstances was to make sure she completed the remaining three-year study and obtain her degree as originally intended. But Deidre could even stretch her imagination further. While raising her growing family, Deidre had taught piano lessons on an occasional basis. She was gifted and had mastered the skill before she got married. Over time, she discovered that she really enjoyed teaching music to kids. So, when Deidre was on the verge of re-conceiving her dream, another option came to mind. She would be taking a combined Bachelors degree in Music and Education. That option would be employing the strength of her modified circumstances with a sense of purpose she had gleaned from those occasional piano lessons she taught. Deidre felt that pursuing this higher goal for her re-conceived dream would be better for her in the long run.

    Just like Deidre, do not lower the ceiling of your desire when you re-conceive your dream after an interruption. Aim at pursuing wilder dreams than you originally intended.

WHAT WILL AN IDEAL FUTURE LOOK LIKE?

Conception of your dream involves a process of envisioning. Whether your dream was interrupted or it is the first time around, you need to be able to cast a vision of what you actually desire. Visualize what your life will be like if in two years from now you realized your interrupted dream. Imagine yourself in that position or situation that bringing forth your dream will create. Imagine what it will be like if you completed that college degree, have a great family relationship, or achieve financial independence. After you have a visual perception of a great future, ask yourself what it will take to move you from where you are to where you desire to be.

Envisioning is the mind's ability to see beyond the ordinary; the ability to go wild with your imagination, the ability to see where you would like things to be in your life. Envisioning requires a mindset that believes in the seemingly impossible. Anyone who is in the right frame of mind, looking past the limits, can cast a vision.

As envisioning is a thing of the mind, one does not even have to have perfect eyesight to have an extraordinary vision. The story of Erik Weihenmayer demonstrates this important fact

THE POWER OF VISION

Erik Weihenmayer is a man with great vision. Ironically he does not have perfect eyesight. In fact, Erik is blind.

Erik was born in 1966 with a disease called retinoschisis which totally claimed his eyesight by the age of thirteen. Erik was determined from this early age to rise above the challenges of his disability. His family played a supportive role towards him reaching this goal.

Erik never let the barrier of perfect eyesight interfere with his passion for having an exciting and fulfilling life. He has performed many seemingly impossible feats and played many different roles. Such roles include being a middle school teacher and wrestling coach, acrobatic skydiver, skier, marathon runner, long distance biker, ice climber and scuba diver.

The extraordinary thing about Erik is the fact that he had the power of vision which was translated into an unimaginable dream. Erik had a dream of 'conquering' the Seven Summits, the highest mountains in each of the seven continents. The dream required him to climb to the summit of each of the seven mountains, and one by one, Erik did exactly that. On September 5, 2002, when he stood on top of Mt. Kosciusko in Australia, he completed his 7-year quest to climb the Seven Summits. With this accomplishment, Erik joined only about 100 people worldwide to have done this. Also, at age 33, he was one of the youngest.

A STEP-BY-STEP APPROACH

The first of Erik's 'conquest' was in 1995, when he reached the 20,320' summit of Mt. McKinley, North America's highest peak, sponsored by the American Foundation for the Blind.

In 1997, he climbed his second continental summit, Kilimanjaro. It was during this climb that Erik got married to his wife Ellen at an altitude of 13,000 feet.

In 1999, he attempted Argentina's Mount Aconcagua. However he and his team had to turn back due to poor weather conditions just short of the summit. Thus, Erik also faced some interruptions in the course of his seven-year feat.

Erik was not to give in. He kept at his dream and he was successful on a second attempt to summit this mountain.

In 2001, Weihenmayer climbed Mt. Everest, becoming the first blind man to reach the summit of this world's highest peak. Erik's Mt. Kosciusko summit in 2002 was the last of the seven summits he had gradually 'captured'! That is indeed a great achievement for a blind man. And Erik would not have been able to perform this step-by-step feat without the power of vision!

Despite his health-related obstacle, Erik's power and vision was translated into his strength to deliver his dream. This strength to deliver continues to multiply in his life as he delivers other leisure and personal development dreams. The strength Erik has acquired also pours out into other areas of his life. Erik has led an expedition to Tibet where he offered leadership to blind teenagers from the Braille Without Borders School.

Weihenmayer has also published his autobiography in the book—*Touch the Top of the World: A Blind Man's Journey to Climb Farther Than the Eye can See* (1). He also teamed up with like-minded people to publish another book, *The Adversity Advantage: Turning Everyday Struggles into Everyday Greatness* (2), which appeals to growth and innovation in the business world.

Yes, the power of vision that Erik has is transforming many aspects of his life and is adding up towards his legacy.

RE-ORGANIZING YOUR DREAM IN A NEW CONTEXT

In Chapter 3, I shared my personal story of re-organizing my legacy dream into the context of the new circumstances, which I faced during its pursuit. The process of re-conceiving an interrupted dream involves acquiring a new understanding of your dream based on your modified circumstances. It is important to know what the idea or concept of your dream entails against the backdrop of your current position. When you understand thoroughly the new conception of your dream, it will help you re-modify your actions and re-organize your goals to fit into the realm of the new situation. Attempting to pursue your goals without modifying the concept of your dream based on your old circumstances, might result in a new disaster.

The fact is that over the period of interruption of a dream, an individual often undergoes a dramatic change in their circumstances and environment. Thus, when the dream is re-conceived, the perception of what you originally conceived would have changed.

As I mentioned in Chapter 3, it is often difficult to predict how long the interruption period for a dream would be. For some dreams, the interruption period could be as long as forty years. That is the case for the dream conceived by Moses, a popular hero and leader from Biblical times.

A DREAM MADE BLUNT BY 40 YEARS IN THE WILDERNESS

Moses is known as the great leader of the Israelites (3). He accomplished so many feats that the testimony of his life reads: *there is no man like Moses on the face of the whole earth.* But for Moses, life was not always filled with such exploits and achievements. In fact, in one phase of Moses' life, the only adventure he had was with cattle and sheep.

• **STRENGTH TO CONCEIVE** •

Moses was destined for greatness. He was raised in the palace and known to be a prince, the son of the Pharaoh-king of Egypt. However in the early part of his life, he discovered his true heritage. He discovered that he was neither an Egyptian, nor the son of the Pharaoh. When he became aware of the fact that he was actually a Hebrew, it made a whole world of difference to his perception of life. It set Moses running to fight for truth and justice for his people, the Israelites. At that time, the nation of Israel was under Egyptian bondage. The Israelites were slaves to the Egyptians and the terms of service were very harsh. So, Moses conceived a dream of an ideal future for himself and his people. The ideal future for the Israelites would be a free world; a world where they would no longer be under the Egyptians' rules or subjected to slavery. Moses' dream of the ideal future was a world where Israel was liberated, free to live the way they wanted and serve their God without hindrance. Moses' dream was that of public service, which would leave a legacy of freedom for his people. Moses conceived the idea and set out to execute it the way he understood it could be done at that time. He killed an Egyptian who he found to be oppressing one of his Hebrew brothers. That particular course of action set up a chain reaction that eventually led to Moses being sent into the wilderness. He became like a cast-away and could not be among his people any more.

Beaten and battered during his wilderness journey, Moses ended up in the strange land of Midian, where he set up his living quarters. He settled down to a new life with the family he acquired in this new land. His dream of liberating the Israelites seemed no longer real to him. In fact, his concept became just a foggy notion he once had as the years passed by. One of the key facts in optical medicine is that poor vision is often due to a change in central vision or the ability to focus. Surrounded by herds and living a nomadic life, Moses' central vision and focus had changed significantly. His poor vision of his original dream was due to the change in his central vision and focus on life.

DIVINE STIMULUS TO REVIVE A LEGACY DREAM

However, and through divine intervention, Moses' dream was resurrected. This was about forty years after his original attempt at delivering his dream. The events of forty years had dulled his perception of an ideal future for his people. Moses was no longer sure of the role he had to play in this unique pursuit. But there was no going back to the particular divine stimulus that Moses received to revive his dream.

Moses had to learn that the renewed vision of his original dream was intertwined with his life's purpose. The vital fact is that when he had his original conception of the dream forty years earlier, his life's purpose had yet to be fully revealed. Therefore, with a new revelation of his life's purpose, Moses' dream became what is referred to as "a calling". The dream would not go away until he fulfilled it. He had accomplished so many other feats like marriage and heroic adventures with his wife's family, yet that was not what Moses' life was about. His life's purpose was to lead the Israelites out of Egypt to the Promised Land.

So how did Moses re-conceive this vital dream in the context of his new circumstances and situation? Moses had to review the divine calling in the light of his new circumstances. He gave a number of reasons that showed that his understanding of the dream had changed. He now had a family and was living in a far away land. The profile of the people he had to lead was different from the Hebrew population of forty years ago. Most importantly, the action plan that he received from his divine stimulus required him to go and talk to the Pharaoh. That was not the pathway Moses had envisioned for executing his dream originally. He suddenly realized the skills needed to execute his revised dream were drastically different from what he originally envisaged.

There were many issues that Moses had to consider in his new conception of the dream. But with more divine affirmation, Moses moved forward with his new role. He eventually brought forth the dream of liberating the Hebrew from the Egyptian's subjugation. However, the full story demonstrated that Moses had to re-conceive his dream, clarifying the vision of the ideal future along the way. He had to constantly re-organize his goals and action plans to fit into the modified situation he often faced in the pursuit of his revived dream.

Many other people in contemporary times have used similar principles to re-conceive their modified dreams in the context of their new circumstances.

FINDING IT DIFFICULT TO RE-CONCEIVE YOUR INTERRUPTED DREAMS?

What are you to do if you are having some difficulty in casting a vision of your ideal future? What happens if it seems impossible to clarify what you really want? There are some types of assistance you could use towards re-conceiving your dream. However, before you consider alternative options, it will be worthwhile to go through a physical and mental check of your situation first.

The list below is a summary of some checks you could perform to ensure that you are able to go through the conceptualizing and envisioning processes of your dream.

Physical checks

Just like medical practitioners advise would-be pregnant mothers to watch their habits, you need to take a similar cue when it comes to re-conceiving your dream.

- Stop habits that reduce your chances of casting an image of an ideal future. Watch what you consume in terms of your environment.
- Do not exert yourself. Getting stressed out will leave you with less energy in the area of your vision-casting process.
- Remove any physical items that might prevent you from re-conceiving the dream. If necessary, change your environment.
- Put in the range of your central vision, items or events that will help your mind grasp different stimuli towards the ultimate delivery of your dream.
- Associate with people that will help you attain the goal you are trying to envision. As mentioned in Chapter 5, this may involve breaking off some relationships that are not helpful and taking on new ones that are more beneficial.
- Beware of fakes. Do not use physical or intellectual resources that are not authentic. Make sure you go for real resources in your goal of conceptualizing your image of an ideal future.

Mindset checks

When it comes to giving birth naturally, most women have some degree of anxiety over the process. Medical studies have even identified an extreme situation whereby some women are scared to death of childbirth. These women are known to be tokophobic and would not even consider the idea of getting pregnant in the first place.

As a result of their extreme fear, some of these women will use up to three methods of contraception simultaneously just to avoid getting pregnant. The irony is that most of the sufferers of this condition confess that they would dearly love to have children. Psychologists ascertain that this incongruity has to do with the women's mindset.

In terms of re-conceiving your dream, you need to have a mindset check. You need to get over any fear or issues that generate fear over the process of pursuing a dream. If such fears are related to the process of delivery, or the energy required in the end stages of the dream, you need to re-assure yourself that you have the ability to perform. You need to be assertive; affirm to yourself that you are able to realize this dream as you set out to re-launch new action plans and goals towards it.

If your dream was previously interrupted at any stage of its growth, you need to be confident that you are capable of moving it forward up to the delivery point this second time around. As mentioned earlier in the chapter, if there are issues with your identity or self-esteem ensure that you resolve them.

The physical and mental checks listed above are initial steps towards solving issues associated with conceiving your new dream or re-conceiving an interrupted dream. But what happens when there is a problem with your ability to conceive naturally? What are you to do if you are finding it difficult to perform those mental and physical checks yourself? How can you get more help, if need be, towards conception of your interrupted dreams?

USE OF ASSISTANCE IN CONCEPTION

I made mention earlier of the fact that the capacity to conceive a baby is not a given for everyone. There is a minor proportion of the population who, for various reasons, lack the ability to get pregnant. According to the National Centre for Health Statistics, in the United States about 12 percent of women (7.3 million) in the United States aged 15-44 had difficulty getting pregnant or carrying a baby to term in 2002 (4). One in six couples worldwide experience some form of fertility problem, leading to problems for women to get pregnant. In terms of male and female fertility factors, both men and women account for 40% of infertility cases; 20% of infertility cases are due to a joint problem (5).

For this naturally infertile group, the number of options available has escalated over the course of the 21st century. There is a wide array of assisted reproductive technologies (ART) available and many couples are tapping into it.

When it comes to conceiving or re-conceiving your dream, you might find that trying hard is not enough. It could be an issue analogous to a physically dead womb that needs some alternative method of growing the foetus. Or it may have to do with deficiencies in other parts that constitute the whole process. Whatever the reason for the difficulty, you may need extra help from outside resources. The following section deals with using assistance to conceive or get clarity with your new or previously interrupted dream.

The types of assistance you could use come under two groups:
- Professional help through coaches and mentors;
- Collaboration with joint venture partners.

These types of assistance could be used at different points of pursuing your dream. They could be used as you re-conceive your dream or as you grow and facet it and at the time of delivery.

COACHES AND MENTORS

If you are finding it difficult to re-conceive a dream, the first thing to do is to check your mental mindset towards attaining your goals. To do this, you might need the help of someone who can support you by asking you powerful questions that can offer you new perspectives. Life coaches are professionals who can help you in this regard. Coaches can help you stretch your imagination when it comes to envision your concept and reframing your situation so you could see it in a different light. As mentioned in Chapter 4, you can locate the help of a professional towards this goal through the International Coach Federation.

Mentors are another group of people who could be of assistance to you in the re-conception of your dream. A mentor is someone who believes in you and is ready to help you achieve your potential through some support. In most cases, a mentor has already been through the path you are currently trying to travel. A mentor has realized a dream similar to the one you are trying to re-conceive. A mentor may be able to direct you to resources where you can get more help towards achieving specific dreams. A mentor can be any one within your circle of influence—family, career or social groups.

COLLABORATION WITH JOINT VENTURE PARTNERS

You could also get assistance towards re-conceiving your dream through collaborating with people with similar goals and interests. Ask yourself; is there someone or some association, some organization with congruent interests that I can collaborate with to achieve my goals? Congruent interests are those that work well together for both parties involved. The interests are similar but not identical. When choosing your joint-venture partners it is important that the collaboration works for the good of each of the parties involved. A good collaboration will not impede your right to re-conceive and move forward in another direction at a later date. Such collaboration will involve you carrying out parallel but different actions concurrently with the partner that will lead you to the ultimate delivery of your dream.

For such collaboration to work effectively, it is essential that you re-conceive the dream together with the partner of choice, so that each party is very clear on what is involved.

ANNOUNCING YOUR DREAM CONCEPTION

You have been able to re-conceive your interrupted dream or conceive a new one. You are pregnant with your new vision of an ideal future. You are so excited about it. You can see things clearly now, more than you ever did when you originally attempted it. You feel like telling everyone you meet all about your new idea.

How are you to proceed announcing your vision of an ideal future to people in your circle of influence?

It is amazing how vast the differences are in the way people from various cultures announce a new pregnancy. At one extreme are cultures that do not favour any form of announcement. People just get to know that a woman is with-child when they see her protruding belly at later stages of the pregnancy. At the other extreme are cultures that celebrate new pregnancies with a huge party a few weeks after a positive hormonal pregnancy test.

Translating this into the case of your new dream conception, ways of announcing your new idea is as varied as the type of dream and the people you intend to inform. Nevertheless, it is essential to exercise some wisdom in the process of publicizing your vision of an ideal future. As mentioned in Chapter 2, your dreams could be so big and so unimaginable that you might be met with scorn or disbelief when you share it with others. You have to be discerning in terms of with whom to share your new dream concept. You have to be astute in knowing when to share the concept that is keeping you awake at night.

Whichever way you decide to go about it, announcing your new vision to others could be the first step towards accountability on the pursuit of your dream. For instance, you need to have some people know that you have a new relationship dream such as engagement to your new love. It is necessary to let some people in your circle of influence know that you have a new conception of re-starting your interrupted college education. Those announcements are ways of saying that you are taking responsibility for your decision. It implies your willingness to fall through in the pursuit of your goals.

Announcing your dream or vision of an ideal future also prepares you for turning your thoughts into action. For example, when a new fiancée announces her engagement to her girlfriends, the first she is asked is, "Have you set a date yet?" It gets you ready for planning actions steps and goals towards bringing forth that dream. That process of growing your dream through thoughtful actions and goals is the subject of the next chapter.

CHAPTER 7

Strength to Grow
Working towards proper development of your dream

TRANSFORMING THOUGHTS INTO ACTION

The first trimester stage of pregnancy is filled with mixed emotions. On the one hand, the expectant mother is very excited about the new gift of life that is growing in her. On the other, it is a period when she has to deal with balancing her life in terms of the old and the new.

In this period of about 13 weeks, the woman experiences the first set of changes in her body due to the effect of the conception. Such changes result in major symptoms of nausea and morning sickness. The baby experiences a significant change too, growing from an egg stage to a length of about four inches.

In terms of your dream pregnancy, during the first trimester you transform your thoughts and ideas into action. Just like every first phase of growth, the period of taking the first set of action steps towards your dream is a critical one. It is a period that makes or breaks the dream.

Those goals that you set at the initial period of your dreams' growth go a long way to determine your success in delivering the dream.

There is however, a critical step to take before you can set realistic goals towards realizing of your dream. You need to determine your target date for delivery.

ESTABLISHING A DATE FOR BRINGING FORTH YOUR DREAM

In Chapter 6, I discussed the issue of announcing that you are pregnant with a concept of an ideal future. A probable reaction to your announcement is a follow-up question regarding the date at which you expect the dream to be realized. Just like an expectant mother, you might be asked to share the expected date of delivery (EDD) of your dream.

Even without being asked, it is important to determine your due date based on your vision of the ideal future. It is essential that, once you have re-conceived your dream, you be very clear as to when you desire to bring it forth.

Setting a due date will be important in the number of action steps you take towards accomplishing your dream as well as the timing of each of those steps. If you cast a dream of financial independence while still obtaining your first degree as a 22-year-old, it makes sense to set a time when you would love this to be achieved. Without a due date, there will be no reasonable planning and you may not be motivated to launch out effective action goals. The goals you set for yourself if you want to bring forth the dream of financial independence at age 30 are different from the goals that you would set if you wanted to realize the dream at age 45.

The other noteworthy point about setting a due date for your dream is the fact that you are the one who sets the due date. Allowing someone else to set a date for your dream delivery implies that you are not taking full ownership of the responsibility for the dream. In that case, if you do not accomplish the goals, you might have an excuse. However, if you set the due date yourself, you will be stimulated to set action goals in line with the timing.

When you set your EDD, recognize that apart from internal factors, there are external variables to consider. Know how to weave each of these factors into the timing so that they work to your advantage.

With a set due date, you are able to progress towards proper development of your dream. You are in the right frame of mind to manage your gestation period. That process begins with some further planning.

LIFE PLANNING

Life planning is a process whereby you write out your dreams and set out action steps and goals towards achieving them. It involves writing the plans for all of the dreams you intend working on, now and in the future, in such a way that you can prioritize your action steps at any given point in time. Therefore, your life plan is an overall view of all your major goals. When you write out a plan for your reconceived dream, you include all of the goals towards achieving it as well as the action steps to take towards attaining each of those goals. During this process, you are transforming your thoughts into actions.

Just as with any other process in the growth of your dream, you need to take ownership of this aspect. You have already set your target due date. In a similar manner, you are also in charge of writing out the plan for making that due date real. You understand and know yourself better than anyone else. You perceive what your life's purpose is and you can weave that plan into it. In addition, writing the plan yourself gives you more motivation towards fulfilling those goals.

LAUNCHING 'SMART' GOALS AND ACTION STEPS

Alyssa had re-conceived her dream of mastering her piano skills. She had a much clearer concept of the dream than when she had abandoned it five years prior to the time of reviving it. When she abandoned her dream, she was only able to play popular, low-level music in restricted settings. In the process of reviving this dream, she had envisioned to master her skills to a level which would enable her to play concert-level music to a much wider audience. Then she decided to set a measurable goal to define what 'mastery' meant in her case. She decided that passing the Royal Conservatory of Music's Grade 10 certificate exam was this measurable target. Moreover, at the forefront of Alyssa's mind was the major reason for picking up this previously abandoned dream. She had discovered that performing in an outreach band would help her fulfill her life's mission of 'shining light onto others'. This fact gave her a renewed sense of purpose and she set out to write a plan for bringing forth her dream of mastering the piano.

Firstly, Alyssa set a due date of 4 years hence for her dream of acquiring the Grade 10 certificate. That meant she had a period of 4 years to complete all of the action steps. With this in mind, Alyssa decided to break the steps into smaller ones. She identified where she was presently—a grade 6 certificate level. For her to Get to Grade 10, she had to move through grades 7, 8, and 9 first. Accordingly, Alyssa set out interval dates to achieve each of these grades. Her date for the Grade 7 was six months from the starting time. Alyssa then took that first goal of obtaining her grade 7 certificate and broke it further down into smaller action steps. Those steps included hiring a piano teacher and scheduling the time for the lessons. Further action steps included allocating at least one hour every day for practice. Now, Alyssa had a complete plan towards bringing forth her dream of obtaining a Grade 10 piano certification.

Here are some highlights of Alyssa's plan:

Alyssa's Plan

Description of dream:
Mastery of piano skills up to Grade 10 Certification
Today's Date: November 20, 2011
Due Date of Dream: December 10, 2015

Table 3.1—Alyssa's Plan for Mastery of Piano Skills

Goal	Action steps	Due Date	Insert a tick when completed	Comment
Grade 7 certification	Hire a piano teacher	Dec. 30, 2011		
	Start piano lessons	Jan. 10, 2012		
	Sit for mock Grade 7 exam	Jun. 10, 2012		
	Sit for actual Grade 7 exam	Jul. 10, 2012		
Grade 8 certification		Aug. 10, 2013		
Grade 9 certification		Sep. 5, 2014		
Grade 10 certification		Dec. 10, 2015		

Alyssa's plan is an example of how you can set SMART goals and action plans towards realizing of your dream.

SMART is an acronym that means:

S—*Specific*
M—*Measurable*
A—*Agreed upon*
R—*Realistic*
T—*Time sensitive*

For instance, the goal of attaining a grade 7 certification by the end of six months is specific, measurable and time sensitive. The goal is realistic because considering the amount of resources she is going to put into it, the allocated time to reach this first goal is sufficient. For Alyssa to set up a goal of obtaining her final grade 10 certification in six months would have been unrealistic. However, since the grade 7 certification is the first of the four different levels she had to attain, setting six months as a due date was realistic.

When setting action steps, it is necessary to have some accountability partner to help you towards keeping up to what you intend to carry out. Alyssa may have chosen a friend or family member to remind her of her goals from time to time. In that way, the goals become agreed upon.

Thus, writing a plan containing SMART goals and action steps is a good tool for working towards proper development of your dream pregnancy.

ON HAVING THE RIGHT DIRECTIONS

When you set out to write a plan for bringing forth your dream, it is essential that you have the right directions. Part of the planning process requires you to find out relevant information that will help you in creating meaningful goals. Do not make assumptions based on hearsay. Neither should you rely on the wrong information. That would be equivalent to using the wrong directions and you would probably end up somewhere else. Going in the wrong direction would lead you to a place you did not plan to go. For instance, Alyssa could have assumed that the grade 7 exam was available all year round in her location. Maybe that type of exam schedule was prevalent when she abandoned the dream five years earlier. However, the correct and current fact may be that the exam is only available once a year at all locations. What's more, the exam date for that year may have passed. An erroneous assumption such as this would have seen Alyssa unable to satisfy that goal for another year.

On the other hand, wrong directions may lead to a waste of your time, energy and efforts as you may find yourself going round in circles. Eventually, you may find yourself at the same spot where you started. You have traveled a long distance and have arrived nowhere different from the beginning of your journey. That strategy will not work towards achievement of your goals.

If you are writing a new life plan for a dream that you previously attempted, it would be wise to take a new approach to your action steps.

A NEW APPROACH TO YOUR ACTION STEPS

In Chapter 5, I discussed the need to do some stock taking when you are reviving a dream that was previously interrupted. The lessons you learn from that exercise should be carried forward both in the process of re-conceiving your dream and in launching new action steps. It is wise to try a new approach to the execution of the steps towards achieving your dream.

Do not get stuck using the old methods that you previously tried to no avail. You have acknowledged that those methods did not work, so you need to be creative and design new approaches. Remember, if you always do what you've always done, you will always get what you've always gotten.

SMART GOALS LEADING TO AN EFFECTIVE CAREER CHANGE

Setting SMART goals and action steps will give you an edge when it comes to growing your dream from the conception stage to the point of delivery. It is a universal concept when it comes to dream fulfillment, being applicable to any category of dreams.

Here is the story of a young woman who tapped into the power of careful planning to grow her unimaginable dream. She did not rest on assumptions but sought out relevant information so she could follow the proper course and directions in transforming her concept into actions. The SMART goals she launched ensured the proper development of her dream, enabling her to bring it forth as a healthy new venture. She used the same principles when it came to nurturing her newly delivered dream, resulting in even more growth to the point of multiplication.

HOW MANY FOOT TAPS DO YOU NEED TO STIMULATE A CAREER CHANGE?

The story of Taryn Rose (1-4) is very unusual. She spent a considerable part of her youth and young adult life working towards a career goal. It was a highly desirable career, especially as it followed her original dreams and 'fit' into the tradition and expectations of her family. Taryn went through the rigours of medical school training, graduated and was finishing her residency as an orthopaedic surgeon, when Taryn had the 'queer' brain wave and foot taps that changed her life and career direction.

Taryn had always loved shoes and used to wear heels to the hospital. However, she never found the right kind of stylish shoes with heels that could support the long hours of standing, which she put in during the course of her work. In short, Taryn wanted to find stylish shoes with heels that would not destroy her feet.

Since she could not get what she desired, Taryn had this unique idea of actually creating them herself. As I mentioned in Chapter 2, this is another example of a dream arising out of the desire to fulfill our human needs. In addition to the need, from her surgery background, Taryn had insider information to an overlooked worldwide problem and decided to buy into it.

Hailing from a family that would rather see her following the career of a surgeon, Taryn faced some barriers when she announced that she was 'pregnant' with this strange dream. Apart from objections from her physician father, she also had to worry about peer opinions and similar issues. However, Taryn felt she was onto something and she feared regret more than failure. So she held onto her dream concept and decided to follow through with it.

FROM AN ORTHOPAEDIC SURGEON TO A SHOE DESIGNER

Her vision was to create shoes that felt good and looked good.

To turn this strange idea into actions, Taryn started off with some research. She turned to her favourite sales clerk at Barneys (an upscale department store) who had friends in the shoe industry. Then she launched SMART action steps and goals based on her vision and the information she had gathered. Taryn applied and got a $200,000 Small Business Administration loan. These essentials steps equipped Taryn with strength to grow her dream. She used the loan and her industry connections to produce her first line of luxury shoes. Growing the dream gradually with more action steps and goals, Taryn was able to bring forth her dream in 1998. She launched her shoe design business with her first line of designer shoes.

Thus, Taryn had the strength to deliver her dream of a unique career change. She interrupted her original career goals and re-focused the context of her life's mission from fitting crushed and broken toes, ankles and insteps to providing the right shoe fittings for sore feet. Using SMART action steps, she re-directed her intellectual efforts from foot surgery to foot fashion.

Over the years, Taryn has not only delivered that new dream, she has nurtured and provided for it. Taryn did a lot of campaigning for her shoes in very relevant markets of high-end buyers and gradually her sales soared. Taryn's hard work and persistence resulted in her dream being multiplied as she further expanded her business. She opened several boutiques including one in Seoul, Korea. She also gradually added on men's shoes and handbags to her collection.

Taryn Rose International has grown considerably over the years into a multimillion revenue company. In 2005, at age 38, Taryn won Fast Company magazine's Top 25 Women Business Builders Award.

Taryn could look back with no regret to the moment she made the decision to follow her heart. Her willingness to follow her dream despite its weirdness has paid off in unforeseeable proportions. Taryn had the courage to challenge the status quo. She stood firm in her belief and refused to be inhibited by key players in her life. This frame of mind had equipped her with the strength to grow, protrude, bring forth, celebrate, provide and multiply her dream. It has given Taryn the strength to deliver her new life's mission.

GIVING AND RECEIVING FEEDBACK

When a woman is expecting, it is a normal procedure to schedule regular visits to the doctor or midwife. Such visits are important in checking and monitoring the growth of the baby and the health of the mother. It is during such appointments that the practitioner offers feedback advice to the woman based on the results of the tests performed. When it comes to proper development of babies, it is essential that the pregnant woman follows the guidelines set out by the medical practitioners.

In a similar manner, during the growth phase of your dream pregnancy, it is important that you perform evaluations on the action steps and goals towards realizing your dream. This is important so that you can identify any issue or concern that may pose danger to the continuity of the growth of your dream. Such periodic checks will help you remove any negative influences and re-direct your efforts towards more beneficial factors.

PERIODIC CHECKS ON THE GROWTH OF YOUR DREAM PREGNANCY

On a periodic basis, perform an evaluation of the growth of your dream. Ask yourself these questions:

- What are the things that get in my way of pursuing the action steps and goals?
- Are there any factors that drain me of energy and prevent me from performing the action steps I planned out?
- Do I need to get rid of some stuff or call off some relationships?
- Should I be doing more of some things?
- Are there things I should stop doing?
- Is there any routine that I need to adjust, ensuring that my dream makes it through this stage?

Providing answers to these questions will help you understand the signals in your environment as they relate to the progress you make in attaining each of your goals. And while being sensitive to your environment, you need to know when to change tactics, if and when necessary. These periodic evaluations will help you identify issues that hinder you from performing your action steps and possible ways of overcoming them. It will also help you identify beneficial factors and feasible means of using them to enhance the growth of your dream.

THE GREATEST RISKS TO DREAMS ARE IN ITS BEGINNING

Although risks are associated with every day living, some events are more prone to risks than others. For human pregnancies, it is established that the greatest risk for spontaneous abortion or miscarriage is during the first trimester (5-6).

In terms of the growth of your dream, it is also a fact that a dream in the early stages of growth faces great risks. Working on your new set of action steps effects a change in the way you used to live. As human beings tend to resist change, it is easy to fall back into what you perceive as 'normal'. Just as for other change events, pressure has to be applied in the same direction continuously to maintain any change you try to achieve. Therefore, it is important to keep working on those action steps and goals. Do not give up if you are feeling any 'nausea' due to changes in your circumstances.

In other instances, your resistance to change may be the inability to give up some of the things you used to do prior to your dream pregnancy. When such things pose danger to the growth of your dream, not giving them up may result in its death. This issue can be compared with that of a pregnant woman who does not follow the advice of her doctor to give up extreme sports or excessive alcohol during pregnancy. Such a woman faces a higher risk of spontaneous abortion or the death of her baby before term. Therefore, in order to give your dream a better chance to develop, it is vital to give up items that present a danger to it.

In addition to our attitude towards change, there are other factors that could cause spontaneous abortion of your dream pregnancy. Such include a short-cut frame of mind and a need for immediate gratification. Do not focus on finding short-cuts that will lead to instant gratification. Apart from the risk of failure, such short-cuts will reduce the enrichment of your journey towards the realization of your dream.

So, what other steps can you take to ensure that your dream does not get aborted in the early stages of your pregnancy? What should you do to ensure that your dream moves from one stage of growth to another?

SETTING PRIORITIES IN YOUR SMART GOALS

One important factor that can kill a dream is a 'toxic' overload of priorities. When you set out to write a plan towards bringing forth your dream, you should prioritize your action steps and align your goals with the dreams you have in other areas of your life. If you take on too many responsibilities at once, the growth of your dream may stop. In fact, the situation may lead to a total imbalance in your life.

Michelle had a dream of achieving financial independence at age 35. She set up great goals and worked hard towards this unique dream. Michelle, who was a single woman, had a debt of $50,000 in student loan from her college days. Immediately after graduation, she started working at a big corporation and was earning a substantial income. Unfortunately, Michelle lost her good job when the company packed up three years later. Michelle then started her own small business at age 28. She also took advantage of the prevailing mortgage market at that time and purchased a house. Michelle was about three months away from her 30th birthday when things began to fall apart. In fact, she felt quite overwhelmed even with her daily routine. She was not just worried about that dream of financial independence; her life was out of balance and she often wondered whether she was going to make it.

Michelle started with a very good vision of an ideal future. However, she had not set good priorities for her goals and action plans towards making that vision a reality. One of the first priorities Michelle could have set in her plan was to get rid of her student loan. She could have moved some other goals down on her list of priorities.

She could have saved the goal of investing in real estate through a mortgage loan at a later time in her life. Michelle had taken on too much upon herself and set too many demanding goals to be achieved within the same short period. That kind of goal setting tends to lead to miscarriage or spontaneous abortion of a dream concept in the early stages of growth. Michelle had overloaded herself during the dream goal setting. Her goals were not SMART. She needed to have given herself a much longer EDD for the realization of that dream.

When you set your SMART goals, it is indispensable to prioritize your action steps so that your dream does not get killed due to an overload of responsibilities.

REALISTIC GOALS BASED ON YOUR NEW CIRCUMSTANCES

While planning action steps for a dream that was previously interrupted, it is imperative to take into account the factor of your modified circumstances. Recognize that a goal that may have been realistic during your previous attempt might not be so in your new situation. Maybe you had started working towards a spiritual dream of going on a missions' trip as a young adult but never realized it. Upon picking up your dream 15 years later, you need to consider new factors in your modified circumstances when making your plans. It could be that you now have a bigger and more mature family. It could be that your present responsibilities allow you to take only a short time off your career. On the other hand, you could be presently occupying a position that will enhance the prospect of going on a missions' trip with a wider range of resources than you could have imagined 15 years earlier. You need to reflect upon such factors when you are setting new goals for your re-launched dream.

It is noteworthy that being realistic in your goal setting is not the same as capping the limit of the height of your dream. As I mentioned in Chapter 6, your re-conceived dream should be as limitless in its height as when you were first working on it. Being realistic in goal setting has to do with the 'how' and the 'when' of achieving goals. It should not affect the scale of your goals—however grandiose they may be.

CELEBRATE 'IN-BETWEEN' GOAL ACHIEVEMENTS

It is also a good idea to find means of celebrating the success upon reaching the milestones of your smaller action steps and goals during the process of your dream journey. Acknowledging such moments of smaller victories will give you more momentum towards performing the remaining action steps. It will motivate you towards growing your dream further to the next stage. For instance, if you were working on a fitness dream towards losing 20lbs. in a ten month period, you should acknowledge your efforts when you achieve smaller steps towards the bigger goal. You could set up a reward for yourself when you have lost the first 5lbs. This kind of celebration will also serve in meeting your need for gratification.

USE NEW INTERRUPTIONS TO YOUR ADVANTAGE

You have set SMART goals and you are working diligently on your action steps towards bringing forth your dream. Then somehow you experience another delay or interruption. The first question that comes to your mind is, "How could things go wrong again even when I am following the rules?" You need to recognize that some interruptions may be due to circumstances beyond your control. As pointed out in Chapter 2, interruptions are not a one-time event. New mistakes, delays or hold-ups may happen at any phase of your dream's journey. You need to be open-minded about such delays. Always analyze the factors surrounding the interruption and carry the lessons you learned forward. If necessary, use the period of delay to gather more resources towards pursuing your dream when it is time to re-launch it. Such resources may be financial, intellectual, spiritual, or health and fitness related. As illustrated in Figure 2.1, after receiving an appropriate stimulus for reviving the dream, re-draw your pathway through your dream gestation cycle and continue moving forward.

THE MIDDLE STAGE OF YOUR DREAM PREGNANCY

The second trimester of pregnancy is usually regarded as the calmer period of the entire gestation period (7). There is a significant increase in the growth of the foetus. The woman's body has now adjusted to the changes. The morning sickness is gone and the woman feels better generally. The baby's growth, even though enormous, is yet to protrude the belly to an extent of discomfort.

The other great fact about the second trimester is that the images of the baby are now visible. The body features are more prominent. In addition, the baby is more active and the mother can see and feel its movements. In fact, everything is becoming more authentic about the new life growing inside the womb. What's more, the mother is experiencing a calmer period and is able to enjoy this part of her journey.

In terms of your dream pregnancy, the middle period of growth is also one that is more serene and composed. You are now more settled into performing the necessary action steps. The initial conflicts that you might have had at the early stages have now been resolved. You understand your system better and you have witnessed the progress of your dream. You have realized some smaller steps towards your ultimate vision. You have a lesser number of action steps to reach the time of bringing forth your dream. Things are looking good.

CONSOLIDATING RESOURCES DURING THE CALMER STAGE OF GROWTH

This calmer period of your dream pregnancy growth should be used to your advantage. It is the best time to consolidate the resources you need towards the process of bringing forth your dream. It is the time to check on what you might need and are yet to acquire. It may also be necessary to do more re-allocation of your resources towards fulfilling the dream. Just like an expectant woman and her family save more money towards their new baby, you also need to divert more financial and other forms of resources towards the growing of your dream. Such investment of your resources, which you would have otherwise used in other functions, would eventually pay off when you bring forth your dream.

The middle period of growth is also a time to continue with your periodic evaluations of the action steps. Continue to remove energy drainers. Moreover, it is a period when you have the opportunity to enhance influences that are beneficial to the growth of the dream. Advance your dream growth by developing more new strategies that will propel you faster towards the achievement of your dream.

Here is the story of a young woman who did just that.

A PIONEER IN AN ABORIGINAL COMMUNITY

Tania Major (8) is young but has demonstrated a unique strength to deliver her dream of obtaining a university education. In 2002, she graduated with a Bachelor of Arts in Criminology and Criminal Justice from Griffith University, Brisbane, Australia. That does not sound like an uncommon accomplishment until you become familiar with Tania's background. Tania was the only person within her community to complete a university degree; indeed, she was the only one to have successfully completed Grade 12. Tania is a Kokoberra woman from Kowanyama, an Australian Aboriginal community.

Tania Major had achieved something of significance—something that none of her ancestors or community indigenes had ever accomplished. How did Tania perform this status quo-shattering feat? How did she acquire her strength to deliver?

Tania received her stimulus from a role model—Noel Pearson who is an advocate of positive change among Aboriginals. Tania saw Noel on TV when she was about 11. She figured if Noel, an educated black Aboriginal person, who came from a mission, could get out and speak his mind, she could do it too. That was how Tania conceived her vital dream of becoming an advocate in her community. She received her stimulus from someone she could refer to as a mentor. At that time, Tania was attending the school in her Kowanyama community. The tradition was that children from the school would move on to an Aboriginal program in a school in Cairns. That was the status quo.

However, at the right time, Tania was challenged by her brother to step out of tradition and go to school in Brisbane. Tania took up the challenge and at 15 she left the community she had known her entire life and traveled to Brisbane. She recognized that if she really was to attend university (like Pearson) and make something of herself, she needed to move out of her community to get more education. Thus, Tania used the power of the motivation she had received from Noel Pearson to keep moving forward. Tania had the strength to grow her dream. She continued to adopt strategies that propelled her towards bringing forth her dream of community advocacy.

Tania attended Clayton College in Brisbane and she was supported through boarding school by Noel Pearson, her role model. Brisbane was a big change for her and she had to adjust to the higher academic standards. She was a straight 'A' student in Kowanyama, but was only reaching 'D's in Clayton. With more determination and hard work, Tania improved her grades. She recognized that it was her 'opportunity to shine' and persisted in her endeavour. She subsequently moved on to attend Griffith University from where she graduated in 2002.

CHALLENGING THE STATUS QUO

Tania has shattered the status quo of tradition. She has moved beyond the walls of negative beliefs and mindsets that hold people back from progressing. Tania Major has demonstrated the strength to bring forth her education dream. That was a major goal towards her dream of becoming a community advocate. Propelling the growth of her dream concept, in 2002, Tania began to address both national and international forums publicly. She began speaking out on Indigenous and Youth affairs. She spoke on national television on issues such as domestic violence and the welfare of young indigenous people.

Putting her dream idea in the range of her central vision, Tania's voice has become stronger, reaching even a wider audience since her university graduation. In 2004, at age 23, Tania Major was elected to the Aboriginal and Torres Strait Island Commission of Australia (ATSIC), becoming the youngest person ever elected to the body. Through this, Tania has more strength to grow her goals towards her public service dream.

In 2007, Tania Major was named Queensland Young Australian of the Year and Young Australian of the Year. She is currently the Youth Development Project Officer for the Cape York Institute for Policy and Leadership.

Tania continues to demonstrate her strength to deliver in her youth advocacy. She has become a role model not only for the indigenous youth but also for all young Australians.

Just as Tania Major grew her status quo-shattering dream of becoming a youth advocate, you also can propel your dream growth by taking more action steps towards its delivery. With more advanced growth, your vision of an ideal future gets more real. These images of reality enhance your knowledge of the fact that your dream concept is gradually taking shape. With this in mind, you will need to take even more action steps and realize more goals to move your dream farther down the path towards delivery. That is the subject of the next chapter.

CHAPTER 8

Strength to Protrude
Managing extreme growth of your dream

In the previous chapter, I discussed how to move your dream from the conceptual state to one of action. You have carried out gradual action steps towards realizing your dream. Through those action steps, you have realized some of the goals that constitute the dream. Your vision of the ideal future is gradually becoming authentic. However, you are not there yet. You still need to take more action steps before you can bring forth your dream. This new set of action steps will move your dream from the growth stage to one of protrusion.

FROM GROWTH TO PROTRUSION

Growth and protrusion both signify increasing the amount, size or dimensions of an object or body. They describe a process of enlargement or expansion. The difference in the terms growth and protrusion lie in the degree or extent of the increase or expansion.

In growing your dream concept, you are gradually attaining some new successes as a result of the action steps and the SMART goals you have taken towards realizing your dream. Those successes may not be evident to other people. They may only know about them if you or someone else tells them. Using the imagery of childbirth, it is similar to a pregnant woman who is in the early period of her pregnancy—the 1st or 2nd trimester.

With some of the goals being realized, you come to a stage whereby you are ready to move your dream from growing to protruding. The advantage associated with the protrusion period is that you are able to launch new action steps with your already established goals as foundation. Such new action steps could result in new goals being realized in rapid succession. This results in a faster rate of realization of goals towards your dream as compared to during the growth stage.

During protrusion, you need to stretch your imagination even further than you did during the earlier stage. Think of possibilities that may seem way out of reach. Recognize that your current actions, knowledge or skills may not take you farther than you are already. During protrusion you need to be bold, brave, daring and ready to take more risks as necessary.

When your dream is in protrusion stage, it becomes glaringly evident to outsiders that you are onto something. You are on your way to realizing an important dream. Your dream is in a stage similar to that of a woman who is in the third trimester of her pregnancy. To grasp some more insights from this analogy, let us take a brief look at the events occurring in this stage of pregnancy.

• **STRENGTH TO PROTRUDE** •

THE PROTRUDING BELLY

The third or last semester of pregnancy (weeks 24-40) is marked by the most significant growth of the baby (1-2). It gains more weight and accomplishes this at a faster rate than it did in the previous two trimesters. The enormous growth causes protrusion of the belly and it is evident to everyone that the woman is expecting.

The woman becomes increasingly eager to bring forth her baby. She spends extra time in preparing her home and gathering other yet-to-be-acquired resources. In addition, she takes frequent walks to keep fit and performs extra exercises. During this period, many first-time mothers also attend birthing classes that prepares them for the process of childbirth. At the end stages of this phase of growth, the baby shifts towards the pelvic area in preparation for the birth. The woman experiences contractions called false labour pains.

This third trimester of pregnancy is a period filled with great anticipation as well as huge discomfort. The baby's enormous growth causes a number of bodily discomforts for the mother. She finds it difficult to find a good sleeping position. Also, because of the foetus's increasing pressure on her bladder, she has to urinate more frequently. She often experiences backaches, shortness of breath and leg cramps. She also feels vulnerable; having to depend on others to perform some activities she otherwise could do herself.

BULGES AND DISCOMFORTS OF ENORMOUS GROWTH

The protrusion of the last trimester of the growth of your dream has many similarities to that of the pregnant woman. You have worked hard on your dream concept for a considerable length of time. You have put in a lot of effort performing those necessary action steps and realized some goals. All these endeavours have resulted in a significant forward shift to the growth of your dream. You are much farther along the path than you were when you launched your first action steps. In most cases, the time you need to complete the remaining action steps, which will result in the bringing forth of your dream, is less than the total time you have already spent working on the dream. The due date of your dream is fast approaching. It is a moment of excitement as you reach forward with anticipation to bringing forth your dream.

However, the enormous growth of your dream is taking more space than ever. You need to put in a lot more of your resources to follow through. You may feel like that pregnant woman who is experiencing huge discomfort. You are diverting more resources towards the rapid growth. You are spending a greater amount of time in your day performing those new action steps. That will necessarily require you to leave some of your normal routine tasks undone.

The events in the protrusion stage of a dream can be viewed in terms of an actress in a new yet-to-be-launched theatre drama. The period of the few weeks before the play officially opens could be referred to as the protrusion stage. The actress has come a long way from the day she won the audition for the role. She has spent long hours reciting the lines and learning the actions. She has put in a great amount of effort in the initial rehearsals. The whole drama troupe has grown together practicing their various roles. She is excited because the due date of bringing forth her dream of stage performance is getting really close. However, those last few weeks of rehearsals would require much more of her time, dedication and attention to details. They would require her to focus on the tasks of perfecting her lines and playing her role. In order to have enough time in a day to allocate towards this protrusion stage, she may have to hire some outside resources to carry out some of her other routine duties. Doing this may make her feel vulnerable because she has to depend on others to do what she otherwise would have done herself.

Just like that actress, you may be having new issues surrounding the protrusion stage of your dream. Despite your excitement as to the approaching due date for bringing forth your dream, you may be feeling discomforts of enormous growth.

How are you to manage the bulging that the enormous growth of your dream causes? What steps do you need to take to accommodate the tremendous growth during the third trimester of your dream pregnancy? How could you acquire the strength to protrude while keeping sane?

MANAGING EXTREME GROWTH OF YOUR DREAM

A positive mindset is an important asset towards surviving the protrusion stage of your dream. Filled with a mixture of apprehension, excitement and possible discomforts, you need to be in the right frame of mind to manage the challenges of huge growth. One pivotal point is to recognize that the stage is one that will pass. The discomforts will not be there for ever. You just need to be able to command all that is required to move through protrusion and you will be there at the delivery point of your dream.

If you are feeling vulnerable for having to depend on others, have a plan of action to even things out after delivery of your dream. Plan to give back the time you have temporarily taken from other valuable issues such as relationships. If the duty is taking time away from one in which you could use hired-help, then go for it. The financial investment you make towards this will pay off as you move through the protrusion onto delivery of your dream.

Another important factor to consider during protrusion is the reaction of observers who can now clearly see the growth of your dream. Handling the invited or uninvited responses you get from other people requires an element of maturity. Such feedback from people who see your protruding growth could range from the positive affirmation to sheer jealousy and hatred. Some people will be so glad of your accomplishments and offer to help you move it along even faster. Others would rather see that dream die than you bringing it forth. You need to be able to handle all of the various packaging of such reactions.

A GROWTH THAT IS EVIDENT FOR ALL TO SEE

When the growth of your dream is evident for all to see, some of the reactions you will receive are attacks, criticisms and other issues that may serve as hindrances. Such could become obstacles in your pathway of moving your dream from protrusion to the delivery point. Some criticisms could serve as stimulus to help you develop newer strategies for further protrusion. However, some critics are just out to drain your enthusiasm or sink the growth of your dream. Some other reactions could be due to envy from people who wish they had what you have. Some other people may feel you are not entitled to such an achievement because of your age, background and other factors. Recognize that people will always have different ranges of opinion about any issue. You need to hold on tightly to your dream concept and keep at it. Do not allow someone to kill your dream.

• STRENGTH TO PROTRUDE •

Deborah Norville (3-4) is one woman who faced negative criticisms at a period of protrusion of the dream of her career growth. Her story illustrates the fact that you can revive and ultimately bring forth your dream even when it is interrupted at protrusion stage.

A PROTRUDING CAREER GROWTH

Deborah Norville enjoyed her job as a TV anchor very much. As she was into journalism right from her college days, her career started at an early phase of her life. At 19, she had managed to conduct a live interview with the President of the United States.

Over time, Deborah grew her career in various aspects. She moved from the role of a reporter to that of an anchor, first in Atlanta and then in Chicago. In 1987, she moved to national scenes being named as the Anchor of *NBC News at Sunrise*. Deborah continued to acquire more strength to deliver as she grew her career. In 1989, she was named co-host of the *Today Show*. This was a great protrusion in the career of Deborah Norville who was 31 at the time. Her growth was glaringly evident for all to see.

However, Deborah's professional crisis started not long after she got on to this new position. The tables turned. She went through a period of negative press. The media started chastising her on the issue of her new co-anchor position. Deborah had replaced Jane Pauley who had held the position for 13 years. The press carried many negative comments surrounding this replacement.

Deborah was literally caught in the web of two big powers—the people (her audience) and the press. The saying goes, "when two elephants fight, it is the grass that suffers". With low audience ratings because of the negative press, Deborah's job was at stake. In addition, she left to go on maternity leave not too long after receiving negative press. It was during her leave that she learnt that her contract would not be renewed. Overnight, Deborah was unemployed. This was a trying combination of life-changing events for Deborah. She had just become a mother and simultaneously had to deal with the prospect of unemployment. She had to face a mixed interruption in her career goals. She became paralyzed with depression.

Somehow when she reached the bottom, Deborah looked inside herself and found renewed purpose. Her strength of purpose was translated into an appointment that came her way with ABC Radio. Deborah was re-born on the radio and she hosted the show for one year.

In late 1993, Deborah was hired by CBS News as a correspondent for a primetime newsmagazine *Street Stories*. Gradually, Deborah Norville got her strength back to deliver her career goals. She worked her way through a maze of television positions. In 1995, CBS named Norville the host of the highly popular syndicated news and entertainment program, *Inside Edition*, a position she holds today.

Deborah is a woman who had the growth of her career interrupted by negative press. It happened at the protrusion stage of her career growth. However, with a renewed sense of purpose, she was able to regain her strength to deliver as she made her way back to the top again. That strength has protruded her career in new ways since that major interruption.

Deborah Norville has received two National Emmy Awards for her television work. She has also authored a book that draws insights from her experiences during her professional crisis—*Back on Track: how to straighten your life when it throws you a curve* (5).

STRENGTHENING WHAT ALREADY EXISTS

The protrusion stage of a dream can also be viewed as a period for strengthening what already exists. As mentioned above, during protrusion, you use the power of your already realized goals to launch out further actions that will propel the realization of many more goals towards delivering your dream.

The protrusion is again like the growth of the baby in the womb during the 3rd trimester. During this period, the new growth that occurs in the foetus is aimed at strengthening what already exists. By the end of the second trimester of pregnancy, most of the development of the various baby organs has already been accomplished. The third trimester growth aims at the full development of all of these organs. A baby delivered early in the third trimester is termed premature. Many of the body organs cannot function well at this stage. The premature baby has to be 'grown' under medical supervision in special facilities outside the womb. The extra weeks of development between 30 and 40 weeks enable most organs to refine their capability. It allows the organs to grow to the extent where they are able to function normally when the baby separates from the womb at birth. The 3rd trimester is for maturing the baby so that it can live an independent life of its own when it is delivered between 38 and 40 weeks.

REFINING THROUGH MORE PERIODIC EVALUATIONS

In similar fashion as for the baby, the protrusion stage of your dream should be employed in refining the capability of its necessary features. The process of refining requires removing impurities, or removing things that do not function well. It involves ensuring that the final product contains no factor that could cause a malfunction or breakdown.

In Chapter 7, I discussed the use of periodic evaluations during the growth of your dream. You need to continue taking such evaluations during the protrusion stage of your dream. You need more of those in the process of refining. When you carry out those evaluations, you are able to see where those impurities are that may jeopardize the functioning of your dream when you bring it forth.

It is not wise to take short-cuts that will jeopardize the chances of survival of your dream. Do not rush it to the delivery point. Take the extra time required to develop your dream fully by taking the extra action steps towards it.

AN ABUNDANCE OF RESOURCES TOWARDS PROTRUSION

As discussed earlier, the period of protrusion requires a maximal amount of resources. Thus, while protruding your dream it is necessary to have an abundance of all the resources. Abundance means having over and above of what you normally use on a daily basis. You need an abundance of health, financial, fitness and intellectual resources.

The question is how wealthy are you? Do you have enough financial resources? Do you have enough energy to push through each of these action steps?

During the third trimester, a pregnant woman is advised to take more walks and exercise more. This is aimed at having an abundance of physical energy towards the great pushes she will have to give during the birth of her baby. In addition, she needs to continue eating well in terms of quality and quantity.

• **STRENGTH TO PROTRUDE** •

You also need to have the physical energy to push through the necessary action steps towards protruding your dream to the point of delivery. You need to take similar steps by paying attention to your health and diet.

The abundant supply of the resources you need comes from the reserve you have been maintaining over time. Creating and maintaining a reserve of supplies results from maintaining an appropriate frame of mind and managing your lifestyle properly. Acquiring the strength to protrude is easier when placed against a backdrop of a lifestyle of constantly maintaining a reserve of all of your resources.

ELASTICITY—THE ABILITY TO STRETCH WITHOUT BREAKING

Resiliency or elasticity is one other vital quality during the period of protrusion of your dream. Elasticity is the ability to return to an original state after expansion, the ability of a body to recover its size and shape after deformation. Stated in another way, it is the ability to stretch without breaking or the quality of being adaptable.

This quality will help you to face the criticisms or attacks that may come as a result of your evident growth. Being resilient will also help you in challenging the status quo that may be necessary to move your dream farther along its path to delivery. When you are elastic, you are able to use periods of new interruptions creatively, to take unrelated action steps that will enhance your dreams growth. Yes, it is a fact that new delays may occur even close to the delivery point of your dream. However, being adaptable will help you see beyond those periods and keep on being motivated about your goals. It will help you to even stretch your imagination further to the realms of unimaginable action steps and goals. Having this kind of quality is of great importance when it comes to reviving relationship dreams.

REVIVING RELATIONSHIP DREAMS AFTER LOSS OF SPOUSE

Throughout this book, I highlight the fact that interrupted dreams could be in varying categories. One important area of interrupted dreams, which is often very difficult to talk about, is that of the discontinuity in normalcy in our lives due to the loss of a loved one. Being a highly emotional subject, people often do not want to talk about death and its aftermath in the lives of loved ones. However, bereavement is a fact of life and the loss of a loved one is one of the most traumatic of all life-changing events we can experience as human beings.

At times, people perceive the 'interruption' caused by the death of a spouse as final or permanent. It is a fact of life—the life of a widow or widower can never be the same as to the one they had when their deceased partner was alive. There is no way of erasing the memory of a loved one. They have contributed to the surviving partner's present life and to who they are today. That fact will always remain.

However, the loss of a spouse does not mean that the living partner can no longer have a new loving relationship. No, they cannot replace the former spouse, but they can go into a new relationship—even marriage—that is enjoyable and even richer than before. It does not mean they have neglected the memory of the deceased spouse. In fact, the new relationship and marriage may help boost the life of the living partner. In the long run, it may help in building the legacy the deceased partner left behind. That legacy includes the living partner, the children (if any), all of the things they treasured and the goals they worked towards before the loss.

Many people have gone on to re-marry after the death of their first spouses. Their first dream of a marriage relationship was interrupted when that first spouse died. The living partners had to go through varying periods of grief. They had to go through a cognitive acceptance of their loss (6). They had to move on to the stage of emotionally accepting that the loss was real. With time, the living partners could then go through an identity change, discovering and embracing a new identity that helps them move on with daily living (7). The road to grief recovery is always a difficult one and the periods and details of how each individual copes vary from one person to another.

The question is: how does the living partner revive the dream of a new loving relationship after or during recovery? How do they acquire new strength to grow new relationships that ultimately lead to a re-marriage? How do they develop new strength to protrude when they are blending two families with children of different spousal backgrounds?

These are interesting questions. But elaborating on such is outside the scope of this book. There are books that offer advice to people who have experienced loss in this respect (8-9).

However, I find the story of Gary and Kathy Young relevant in the illustration of one salient fact. It demonstrates that it is possible to find the strength to deliver one's dream of a loving family relationship after an interruption caused by the death of a first spouse.

Gary and Kathy Young acquired the strength to conceive, grow and bring forth their dreams of finding a new spouse after they lost their first spouses. They have acquired an enormous amount of strength required to protrude their dream. This strength to protrude has translated into the ability to stretch without breaking as they blended their first families together into one. Theirs is a story of hope.

A STORY WITH TWO PARTS IN ONE

Gary and Kathy Young's story has two parts in one. Gary's first marriage was to Kathie (spelled with 'ie') who died after struggling with breast cancer. Kathy (spelled with a 'y') was Sandy's spouse in her first marriage. Sandy died of lung cancer.

Gary and Kathy went through periods of grieving. On their roads to recovery, they met through a grief support group that both of them attended. They dated, and found a new love in each other. They made a commitment to each other, got re-married and started a blended family.

The intricacies of the story of the Youngs go far more than stated in the previous paragraph. In fact, when Gary and Kathy lost their first spouses, they were discouraged not only because of their losses, but also due to the minimal number of resources available to young widows and widowers. They discovered that, among other things, there was little literature on the topic for people of their age at that time. Having found strength through their experiences of finding new love and starting again, they decided to put their story together in a book titled '*Loss and Found*' (10) released six years after their marriage.

GARY AND KATHIE'S 'STRENGTH AT ITS MINIMUM'

After the loss of their first spouses, Gary and Kathy lost their 'strength to deliver' in many aspects of their lives. As mentioned in Chapter 3, it was a period of strength at its minimum. Gary was 43 when his first wife, Kathie, died in 1988 at the age of 39. They had been married for 20 years and were blessed with two daughters. The grief and accompanying interruption caused by the loss was much more than he could bear.

In Kathy's case, her strength to deliver also plummeted when she lost Sandy in 1991. Kathy, then 39, was relatively young when she became a widow. She and Sandy had three sons together. Kathy, who was an elementary school teacher, became an apartment manager while raising her young children.

After bereavement; the length of the period of waiting before a living partner engages in active search for a new love, varies from one individual to another. It is essential that the process of healing takes place before launching into another relationship. The process of healing could be lengthy. However, Gary and Kathy can testify to the fact that 'even with what might appear to be an insurmountable obstacle, you have the ability to heal yourself' (10).

AN APPEALING DREAM FOR A SPOUSE AND NOT JUST A 'RELATIONSHIP'

Gary and Kathy had a very engaging dream—finding a new spouse, implying marriage, and not just a relationship. They were very clear about what they desired.

What is at stake for this kind of dream? What types of obstacles could they face in the pursuit of this important dream?

Gary and Kathy's dream is not unusual at all and is a highly desirable one. Many older widows and widowers find new love and re-marry (11-12). However, Gary and Kathy were younger than the typical widow or widower. In most cases, such older widows/widowers have retired and their children have all left home. These older folks do not have problems with stretching finances and do not worry about career or the lack of it.

However, these are the kind of issues Gary and Kathy had to worry about. They also had to think about children, nannies, education, in-laws and alike.

THE STRENGTH TO REVIVE 'DATING'

It seems natural that to find a new love one has to go out and date prospects. For Gary and Kathy to grow the dream they had conceived, they had to put on the 'dating' hat again. But there was this awkwardness to deal with. How could Gary start dating after a hiatus of 20 years? And how could Kathy seek out a new love when the last time she did was over 14 years ago?

There was also the factor of their children. Dating with younger children is not the same as dating as when one is 18.

And how are they to shield their children from dating disasters? Or what happens when they finally find someone they love and the kids do not enjoy the company of the newcomer?

Gary and Kathy were able to face their fears squarely and gradually got back into the dating world. Since they met at the grief support group in 1992, Gary and Kathy had become friends. But they did not start dating until later. Each partner had dated a number of interesting prospects. In time, they found in each other a love that was worth pursuing and made a commitment to each other. It was almost too late for that because Kathy had agreed to marry someone else before Gary insisted she was meant for him.

• **STRENGTH TO PROTRUDE** •

When Gary and Kathy shared the news of their engagement with their children, each set was very pleased with the decision. This is a factor that augured well for their relationship.

A CONSOLIDATION OF NEW LOVE

The dream of a new spouse became very real as they chose their date of marriage in the summer of 1995. This was seven years after Gary lost his first wife and four years after Kathy lost her first husband. It was finally happening. Gary was then 50 and Kathy 43. Tying the knot again, which seemed a huge challenge after a period of grief, had come to reality. Gary and Kathy had the strength to bring forth their challenging dream! They also had the unique opportunity to celebrate again with friends and family.

GROWING STEPFAMILIES—STRETCHING WITHOUT BREAKING

The marriage consummated, Gary and Kathy moved into their desired home with their five children. Kathy's three sons from her first marriage were younger than Gary's two daughters from his first marriage; blending these children, some of whom were teenagers at the time, was another huge challenge. It is a well known fact that growing stepfamilies can be stretching. However the Youngs continued to gather new strength to raise their children together while growing their love for each other. They acquired the strength to protrude, to stretch without breaking.

A NEW LIFE'S MISSION

Their experience with grief, grief recovery, dating, re-marriage and blended families has given Gary and Kathy some unique strength and sense of purpose. The strength developed over the course of bringing forth their dream of finding a new spouse has been translated into a life's mission. They desire to help other young widows and widowers who are facing similar situations to what they went through.

Since the launch of their book *'Loss and Found'*, the Youngs have been participating in seminars, equipping young widows and widowers with tools to help them through their grieving and grief recovery. They have also become co-leaders of some grief support groups. They have spoken on TV shows, empowering their target audience with a message of hope.

Gary and Kathy Young continue to demonstrate unique strength to deliver as they help other young widows and widowers to find the strength to bring forth fresh dreams of loving family relationships.

CARRYING OTHERS ALONG WITH YOU IN THE PROCESS OF PROTRUDING

It is evident that moving your dream through a stage of protrusion demands a lot from you as a person. With all the excitement around your successes it is easy to get carried away. It is easy to become self-absorbed with the apprehension of the nearing due date of your dream. It is essential that you do not become so focused on yourself that you are not aware of the needs of others around you. Do not invade other peoples' spaces.

Amidst your busy schedule, do spend time on other peoples' needs. Look for ways of carrying others in your circle of influence along

STRENGTH TO PROTRUDE

with you in the process of your smaller successes. Remember, your dream pursuit is a journey and you should enjoy the process as much as the end results. Helping other people meet their needs along your journey could be a means of enriching your own dream. When you pour out yourself onto others, you will find your own needs being met, too.

You have grown your dream in a tremendous fashion. You are excited by the approaching due date. You have gathered all of the resources you need for bringing forth your dream. After those months or years of hard work towards attaining your dream, the due date is getting close. Your expectations are high. You are ready to demonstrate the strength to bring forth your dream.

CHAPTER 9

Strength to Bring Forth

Releasing your dream to the world

The due date for delivery of your dream is here. The long-awaited moment has arrived. This is the end point you have been working towards for a long time. It is time to realize that vision of the ideal future. It is your moment to consolidate all of your efforts towards one of the last action steps that will launch forth your dream.

It is time to summon the strength you require to bring forth that dream. That strength to bring forth your dream is as desirable as all other forms of strength you had gathered during your journey from conception to this moment. Before you launch out, it is wise to check your readiness for this great event in the life of your dream.

ARE YOU READY FOR THE DUE DATE?

Here is a quick checklist to ensure you are both physically and emotionally ready for the great step of giving birth to your dream:

- Have you completed all of the action steps necessary to ensure maturity of your dream?
- Have you realized the goals related to refining the capability of your dream to ensure it will be functional when released?
- Have you gathered all of the resources needed for delivery?
- Do you have a reserve of physical strength in proportion to the type of dream you are delivering?
- Have you procured help to cover your routine duties when you will be away birthing your dream?
- Have you enlisted support of friends and/or associates as necessary?
- Do you have standby professional assistance if required?

This is a general list and to make the process meaningful, you have to add the details particular to your dream. Consider the case of Jack who had been working on reviving an interrupted relationship dream for the past two years. His concept of the ideal future was to see the relationship between he and his dad restored into a loving one. Prior to the time he re-conceived this vision, Jack had been estranged from his dad for five years. There were many complex factors Jack had to deal with as some other people were involved in the whole scenario. However, with determination and persistence, Jack had realized many goals towards his ultimate vision of an ideal future. He had grown the dream in tremendous ways since he revived it. He envisaged that the consolidation of all of the previous efforts would result in him returning to his home town and resume an enhanced position in his dad's business. To Jack, this event signified the due date of his dream. Thus, Jack's checklist for his readiness to bring forth his dream included the following:

- Re-established relationships with all major parties in his dad's office
- Ensured his wife had a job offer in the same town
- Maintained a high level of physical fitness especially during the last few months before the move
- Procured the help of four friends in view of the imminent move.

Jack needed to affirm that the dream he had been working on for two years would survive when he brought it forth. That required even more planning. In similar ways you need to ascertain your readiness for delivery of your long-awaited dream.

But what actually happens during delivery of dreams? What are the highlights of the event of bringing forth your vision?

To illustrate this, let us glean some insights from delivery of human babies.

GIVING BIRTH NATURALLY

Natural childbirth consists of three stages: contractions, delivery of the baby and removal of the placenta (1). The contractions that the woman experience at the beginning of labour serve to widen the cervix, the neck of the womb. This stage takes from 8 to 13hrs. or even more. During the second stage, the baby is moved through the birth canal by both uterine contractions and additional 'pushing' efforts by the woman. This pushing effort is similar to that of a huge amount of straining required for a large bowel movement and demands a great amount of physical energy. Immediately after birth, the baby undergoes acclimatization to independent breathing. The mother is allowed to breastfeed the baby and this process aids the expelling of the placenta from the uterus. This removal of the membrane, which had held the baby inside the womb, is the final stage of childbirth. It is important that the placenta is expelled whole as any remaining parts may cause bleeding or infection in the mother.

Natural childbirth is a process encouraged by many medical practitioners. However, this is not always possible due to complications during pregnancy or labour. Extreme cases of complication may result in the death of the baby or the mother. Emergency surgical interventions are used to avoid such incidences. This could be either through forceps delivery or a Caesarean section.

Apart from this complication-related need to perform surgical intervention during childbirth, many women are deliberately opting to have their babies delivered through a Caesarean section. They make that choice for surgical delivery right before their due dates. However, many traditionalists will always vow for the natural childbirth experience.

ON TAKING A POSITION FOR YOUR METHOD OF DELIVERY

Just as there are choices to take in terms of which method of delivery is used for human childbirth, you also have a choice to make as regards which way you desire to bring forth your dream. Your choice of methods and means of delivery is as important as the choice you made during all of the other stages of growth of your dream. When you take your position on the issue of the style you desire to release your dream, you are taking full responsibility for the action. That puts you in charge over the process, and this is where you need to be to make things work.

Taking an active part in the method of delivery you desire for your dream pregnancy begins at the moment you conceive the dream. You incorporate this factor into all the action steps you planned when you are growing the dream. If you desire to bring forth your dream naturally, you need to keep fit physically. You need to have included fitness plans in your action steps during the growth and protrusion of your dream.

Whichever method you choose to bring forth your dream, recognize that your aim is to have that dream come out alive. Your goal is to ensure your delivered dream survives through the pushes and rigours of the process. Your ultimate desire is that you, too, are strong, alive and healthy to enjoy your newly delivered dream.

THE TIME TO PUSH IS TIME FOR ACTION

As mentioned above, pushing is the major action during the middle stage of childbirth. Push and breathe. Then there is more pushing. The cycle continues until the baby comes out of the birth canal. That is essentially what you need to do to bring forth your dream. You need to cause your dream to advance by force until it is released. You need to take action by just doing it. You need to use that extra effort or energy to accomplish that final goal that will effect the bringing forth of your dream. You need to extend your action steps beyond the limit which you achieved during the protrusion stage.

You need to force your situation to move from where it was to the point of your ideal future by exercising an enormous push to top what you have already achieved during protrusion. You need to make a sustained effort in your goal achievement until that dream is brought forth.

The time to push is time to push. It requires your full concentration. It is time for quick fast action. Many women who are facing their first childbirth have heard various tales and stories about giving birth before their due date. Some have watched videos of other women going through the experience. However, when the time to push to bring forth their own baby arrives, those tales will have little connection to what happens to them. The time to push is not the time to reminisce about old wives' tales. It is time to act on their own to make sure their efforts result in safe delivery. The time to push is not the time to theorize about the anatomy of the baby's head compared to the birth canal. When the midwife says "P…U…S…H…," the woman needs to P…U…S…H….

The time to push is time to summon all that is required to advance the movement of the dream and launch it into the world.

A FAST ACTION AND A FOCUSED MINDSET IS REQUIRED FOR DRIVING

When my family moved abroad from Africa, I had to re-take my driving lessons. The driving rules were different from those in my home country. Most importantly, I had to learn to drive on the opposite side of the road to what I was used to. To set me on the right path, I used the services of a driving instructor from one of the most popular driving schools in England called the British School of Motoring.

My instructor was a patient man and he was as keen as I was for me to acquire the necessary skills for safe driving. After the first few lessons, he asked me what profession I was engaged in. I did not quite understand the relevancy of the question but I answered all the same. I told him I was a medical research scientist. To my surprise, he breathed a sigh of relief as if he had discovered some vital truth. He then looked me in the eye and told me that if I were to make enough progress in my lessons, which would ultimately earn me a British driving license, I needed to re-orientate my thinking. I needed to stop taking the act of driving as if it were an item of research, which I needed to theorize, experiment first and then act upon.

I needed to drop the theorizing aspect. I needed to stop mental calculation of the speed at which to drive, so I could stop within the range of distance between me and the next vehicle. That approach would not work. It was not practical. Those factors had already been calculated by the car design engineer. All I needed to do was to take in a very quick snapshot of the road ahead of me, put my feet to the gas pedal, and drive (safely) following the road signs. That was, and still is an interesting experience when learning to drive. (I took my instructor's advice, acquired the skills and eventually obtained my British Driving License.)

GIVING BIRTH TO YOUR DREAM REQUIRES YOUR WHOLE BEING

A similar lesson applies to giving birth. I recognize that, in terms of the time and thinking space required, driving is far different from the process of birthing some dreams. However, the principle is similar. The time for giving birth to your dream is time for action. It is time to just *do it*. It is time to concentrate, put your entire effort and attention to it and PUSH. It is time to exert all of the necessary force to effect the release of your dream into the world.

With this amount of stamina, energy and concentration required, giving birth to your dream requires your whole being. Do not let your dream die in the process of birthing. You have come a long way to this point. You need to bring forth that dream by giving that moment all you've got.

HAVING ENOUGH PHYSICAL STRENGTH TO PUSH

Earlier on in this chapter, I gave a checklist of things which should be ready by the due date of your dream. One of the points listed is ensuring that you have a reserve of physical strength. This point cannot be overstated. Even when you have every other item ready, without the physical strength, *pushing* to bring forth your dream may be impossible. Not having the strength to bring forth on the due date may result in dream disasters. Considering the amount of effort you have invested in the dream, you do not want to engage any seeming obstacle to giving birth to it.

The amount of physical strength you need to launch forth your vision of an ideal 'now' depends on the type of dream. Physical fitness dreams such as summiting the Everest will require more energetic pushes than others. What's more, if you are bringing forth twin dreams at the same time, you will require more strength than just for one single dream.

Whatever the category of your dream, you need to maintain a level of fitness required for that due date by practicing way ahead of time. Grasp as much information about the particular process involved in the birthing of that type of dream while you are still at the growing stage. Then, employ a mentor or coach to help you practice the moves many times before the due date of the dream. Practicing before prime time will bring you to the level of fitness required on the due date.

Apart from physical strength, you also need emotional strength in the process of bringing forth your dream. Having a friend or discerning companion to support you through the process is a wise decision. It may just be someone to vent the pain you may encounter during the release of your dream. On the other hand, it could be an ear to serve as a sounding board for a vital quick decision that needed to be made during the process. Such emotional support will help you maintain some sanity through the course of action.

TAKING BREATHERS IN BETWEEN PUSHES

The action time of pushing strongly during the birthing process of your dream requires so much energy that it is essential to take long deep breaths between pushes. This may require you to physically leave centre-stage and just move to an open space to get some fresh air. It all depends on the type of dream you are bringing forth. Find a means of taking a small break to re-vitalize your mind and body for the next set of long pushes. Take in enough air to replace the lost oxygen. It is important to obtain new reserve of energy so that you can push strongly to effect the final release of your dream.

ADJUST YOUR TACTICS TO MATCH A CHANGING ENVIRONMENT

All through the various stages of gestation, it was important to understand or be cognizant of the factors in your environment as it affected your dream. This point is also relevant during the process of bringing forth your dream.

During childbirth, the medical team keeps en eye on the process by monitoring the baby and the mother. At times, during the labour process, the practitioner changes tactics to ensure safe delivery of the baby and the health of the mother.

In similar ways, during the delivery process of your dream, you need to recognize changes in your environment that may signal a threat to your ability to realize the final goal that will launch your dream. You need to have a perception of your delivery environment. You need to be able to pick up signals from people or things and translate them into messages that you understand. Once you have reached this understanding, you need to change tactics if and when necessary. You need to respond appropriately to ensure safe delivery of your dream. This is especially important because anything could happen up to the time of your dream's delivery even up to the last minute before you bring it forth.

Here is the story of a man who held onto his original dream and was able to bring it forth, literally at the last minute.

THE MAN THAT NEVER GAVE UP HIS DREAM

The remarkable story of Daniel Rudy Ruettinger was captured in the movie 'Rudy' (2). Rudy's story has many powerful insights in terms of having the strength to revive and give birth to interrupted dreams. What is extraordinary about Rudy is that it was during the very last minute that he amassed the strength to bring forth his dream. His push was very strong and timely. One more minute and he could have failed in bringing forth the dream. Without that mighty push, the dream could have died and never got fulfilled. His story demonstrates that you should never give up on your dream.

• STRENGTH TO BRING FORTH •

Born in 1948 to a middle class family in Illinois, Rudy had a unique dream right from his youth. The dream was to attend Notre Dame College and play football for the Fighting Irish team. People may wonder why Rudy chose this particular dream, but that fact is irrelevant. As I mentioned in Chapter 6, each individual is at liberty to dream of achieving whatever they like. Each one is free to let their imaginations run wild while casting visions of their ideal future.

Rudy's distinctive dream was composed of two intertwined goals. The first goal was that of attending Notre Dame while the second interconnected goal was playing football for the Fighting Irish. The dream had an education/career and a leisure/personal development component. He had to be able to attend Notre Dame before he could play football for the Fighting Irish. However, if he did attend Notre Dame but did not get to play football with his favourite team, his dream would still be incomplete. This intertwined dream turned out to be Rudy's mission. No matter what else he did, when the dream remained unaccomplished, he did not feel complete.

THE ODDS WERE AGAINST RUDY

However, the fact is that Rudy faced many obstacles, which he had to overcome before he could attain his goal. The odds were against him in the accomplishment of the dream. Firstly, at the outset, his grade point average was too low to qualify him for an admission into Notre Dame. Secondly, even if he was able to make the grade and get admitted into the college, Rudy did not have the right build to qualify him for the team. He was only 5'7" and 165 pounds which is far shorter and far lighter than the required standards for a collegiate football player. Therefore, Rudy's chances to accomplish his dream were very low. Yet, he did not give up. He had clarity of what he wanted and pursue it wholeheartedly, he did!

After high school, Rudy attended junior college but dropped out because of low grades. This was a major interruption in his dream. He went to work in a power plant and then moved on and enrolled in the US Navy. It was during a tour-of-duty that Rudy received his stimulus for reviving his dream. His experience in the Navy made Rudy realize that he could actually handle responsibility.

ATTENDING NOTRE DAME COLLEGE

Rudy went back to work at the power plant with more enthusiasm. This time he was more motivated to revive his dream towards attending Notre Dame. He was determined not to listen to the criticisms and negative comments from his friends, family and co-workers. He quit his job and relocated to South Bend where he managed to get admission into Holy Cross College (a college affiliated with Notre Dame). This was the beginning of the growth of Rudy's re-conceived dream. Through hard work and determination, Rudy kept obtaining good grades. Thus, after two years at Holy Cross and three previous rejections to transfer to the University of Notre Dame, Rudy was finally accepted as a student in the fall of 1974—during the final semester of his eligibility transfer from Holy Cross to Notre Dame. So Rudy had 'pushed really hard' to have the strength to bring forth the first part of his dream—attending Notre Dame College.

Rudy entered his dream school six years after high school graduation. The major interruption phase was that long. However, he had grown through the period and was better equipped. While in Notre Dame, Rudy re-conceived his second intertwined dream—

to play football with the Fighting Irish. After many applications and try-outs, Rudy made the team as a walk on, one of the lowest positions offered. Rudy was not discouraged but decided to make the most of this opportunity.

PLAYING FOOTBALL WITH THE FIGHTING IRISH

Now Rudy was getting really close to the delivery point of the second part of his dream—to play football with the Fighting Irish!

In the last game of his senior year (and this was the last game in which he would get a chance to play), Rudy was all ready. His coach put him in the game in the last 27 seconds, after sacking the quarterback! Rudy pushed towards bringing forth his dream and scored a goal at the last minute. It was a play in the only game of his college football career. His team-mates were overjoyed and carried Rudy off the field in celebration. Rudy delivered his dream and his whole team had the strength to celebrate with him. That celebration was unique in that it was the first time in the school's history a player was carried on the shoulders of his team-mates.

Yes, Rudy Ruettinger did attend Notre Dame and he played football with the Fighting Irish.

Rudy 'pushed strongly' and delivered his dream even at the very last minute. It took him over seven years after high school graduation to see his whole dream come true. His dream went through a longer gestation period than expected. Yet, he made it through. All of the interruptions and rejections he faced on the journey to that achievement are now history. What matters now is the fact that he succeeded in achieving his goals.

MANY MORE MIGHTY PUSHES

Bringing forth that dream has spilled into other areas of Rudy's life. The strength and sense of purpose he received from delivering that seemingly impossible dream enabled him to follow other pursuits whole heartedly. One such pursuit is the making of the movie of his life's story. Just like his original dream, Rudy was told this new feat could not be achieved since his story was not particularly exciting to Hollywood buyers. However, he followed through. It took him nine years to see this dream of the movie come to fruition.

Today, Rudy is a motivational speaker, sharing his message of 'Yes, I can' with audiences (3). Rudy had the strength to deliver his dream and he is now equipping others to find strength to deliver their dreams!

Rudy's story shows that your success may be just around the corner of one mighty last push. However, what happens if that mighty push is not bringing forth the dream?

WHAT IS PREVENTING YOU FROM BRINGING FORTH YOUR DREAM?

Dreams can have untold and numerous complications during labour or at the point of delivery. You have tried hard doing it naturally. With all of the determination you could muster and your whole being, you have pushed hard. However, your dream doesn't seem to be coming out. It seems that the dream is stuck in the birth canal. What are you to do to remove any bottlenecks in the birth canal so that your dream can go through and be released to the world?

What you could do at this critical stage of your dream delivery is to employ some professional assistance.

As mentioned above in the checklist for delivery, it is recommended that you have some form of standby professional help on the date of your delivery in case you need it. So, if it does happen that your dream gets stuck in the process of giving birth, you need to use the professional assistance nearby.

USING ASSISTANCE IN DELIVERY

Different forms of professional assistance could help you identify the bottleneck issues that are obstructing the mechanism of delivery of your dream. In addition, they could help you resolve any such issues. Life coaches can be of great help in this regard. They could help you widen your dream birthing pathway so that your dream can be released and you can launch it out. In addition, coaches can also help you towards safe delivery of your dream. They could help you move things along quickly in the final stages, so that your own health is not jeopardized from too much stress.

Mentors are also individuals who could provide valuable emotional support to see you through the scariness of the birthing process of your dream. This group of people could serve as your sounding board while you are making that quick vital decision needed during the birthing process. They could also help you deal with individuals or situations that threaten the delivery of your dream.

If you use the help of a close associate or friend during the birthing process, always ensure that you use a discerning person who is really interested in your goals and success. Use someone who is not competing for an identical end result as the one you are pursuing.

Just as during conception, you could also use a joint venture partner in the process of bringing forth your dream. When you do, always seek out a partner whose goals are not opposed to yours. Engage in joint-ventures with people whose role playing will enhance your set of goals towards achieving your dream. On a similar note, your role playing will serve as an advantage to your partner in reaching his goals. In the end, both parties profit through the arrangement.

Bringing forth dreams requires mighty pushes which, in turn, are relying on a good stamina. But, even a health-related interruption should not deter someone from making significant achievements in life. Marnie Walker is a woman who overcame a health-related obstacle and brought forth her business dream.

RISING ABOVE THE CHALLENGES OF TRADITION AND ILLNESS

Marnie Walker is someone who could not be confined by a negative mindset of tradition or illness. Despite many obstructions in her path, she has been able to demonstrate to the world that she does have the strength to deliver (4-7).

Born in a small town in Ontario, Canada, Marnie's father was a successful entrepreneur. However, he was of the school that believes women do not need to be educated. His belief was that the role of women should be limited to that of being wives, home makers and raising children. This mindset put Marnie in a place where she would have been uneducated and maybe never run a business of her own.

Marnie's challenge in life was not only in the cultural restrictions imposed by her family. At 17, she developed a life-threatening illness that affected her ability to walk. She had to spend eight years on crutches and canes. This was a major-health-related interruption for Marnie. With surgery and therapy, Marnie learnt to walk again.

• STRENGTH TO BRING FORTH •

During this seemingly difficult time of interruption, Marnie stood firm on her belief that she would not be limited by cultural inhibition or illness. She enrolled at York University and became one of the first ten women to graduate with a Masters in Business Administration.

Marnie's strength and sense of purpose developed sharply during her struggles. She carried these into her career life after graduation. After working in business development, marketing and advertising for a number of firms, she decided to look for an opportunity to start a company of her own.

MARNIE TAPPED INTO A NEED SHE CAN RELATE TO

Marnie learnt of the difficulty the School Board was having in transporting children with special needs. Marnie had an insider's view into this problem through her previous experience with the illness. She decided it was a need that she wanted to address as a businesswoman. She saw the possibility that was available in this niche.

Marnie decided to follow her own instincts. Although it was like striking into the unknown, her previous ability in overcoming obstacles earlier in her life gave her some confidence. She conceived a vision of an ideal future whereby she would open and manage such a business. With SMART goal-setting and carrying out more action steps, Marnie protruded her dream.

In 1990, with 8 buses, Marnie established Student Express as a transportation company for children with special needs. This was the birthing of Marnie's dream! She had financed the start-up with her credit card and hired a manager and some drivers. She kept her day job for five years afterwards, and invested everything she had to keep the company going.

The efforts and determination, which Marnie put in over those years, resulted in a great growth for her company. She brought forth more dreams while growing the company. In 2004, the company had 250 buses, employed 292 people and generated over $10 million in revenue!

Marnie's strength and determination helped her wade through many different obstacles to build a successful business that became well recognized by the Ontario Government and corporate bodies.

Marnie Walker had the strength to celebrate her achievements through the many awards she has received. In 2004, she was named the Rotman *Woman Entrepreneur of the Year*, Founder of *Student Express*. In 2005 she was the Canadian Association of Women Executives and Entrepreneurs' *Extraordinary Woman of the Year!*

Marnie sold Student Express in 2005. She is working on a new entrepreneurial venture; a prestigious business centre in the heart of Toronto. Marnie has the strength to deliver despite the initial hurdle of the health problems she encountered in her youth!

CLEANING UP AFTER BRINGING FORTH

As I mentioned above, after childbirth it is essential that the placenta be expelled whole from the uterus. This action is vital to the mother's health thereafter. In a similar fashion, it is necessary for you to remove any unwanted remains from the process of bringing forth your dream. It is necessary to clean up after birthing your dream so that you have a clean environment to start off new dream conceptions. The process of tidying up may mean taking different action steps depending on the type of dream to which you have given birth.

It could be that you realized your dream of launching a new business. During the process of bringing forth that dream, you have accumulated so many scrap documents that they cover one side of your office. Take some time to remove all unwanted materials so that you can have a clean environment. When you have a healthy environment, you will be able to conceive new dreams and multiply your dream fulfillment.

WELL DONE! YOUR DREAM IS BIRTHED!!

You have brought forth your dream. That experience has involved your whole being. The method you used in the delivery is now history. The relevant fact that will remain with you is that your dream has been released to the world. You have realized the ultimate goal. You have established that desired future that your vision depicted. You are no longer the same as you were before. Your life has changed due to your new dream achievement. You should be proud of yourself. You have done a good job! Well done!!

Since you have now realized your long awaited dream, you have the right to feel on top of the world. You are really excited about your accomplishment.

It is time to celebrate!!!

CHAPTER 10

Strength to Celebrate

Taking ownership of your newly delivered dream

Congratulations! You made it. You accomplished your long-desired goal. The vision you cast of an ideal future has become real. That future is now here. What a wonderful moment. It naturally follows that you want to celebrate your achievement. You want to share your moment of victory with friends, associates and family. So you call in for celebrations. You get a party organized. You set up a special event to share your joy.

Unlike other parts of your journey towards the goal you have just realized, the process of celebration does not seem to require motivation. What is it about celebration that makes it so natural?

WHY CELEBRATE?

Having the strength to celebrate is a desirable thing. Here are some good reasons for aiming to discover that strength anew:

(a) Celebration makes your achievement full.

Celebrating is an act of recognition. It is a result of our human craving; the desire to fulfill that human need for acceptance, satisfaction, love and joy. When you celebrate your achievement, others will get to know of it. They will get to know you are capable of great deeds. The moment of celebration helps people in your circle of influence share their thoughts and feelings about your new dream. To be recognized as having all of the desirable properties is a significant aspect of fulfillment.

(b) Celebrating your realized goal is empowering.

Celebrating is a means of announcing the new status you acquired as a result of the delivery of your dream. You are making a proclamation that you are no longer the same as you were before the dream was realized. Thus, celebrating your achievement sanctions and imparts some endorsement. It authorizes you to bear that new title which is the end result of your achievement. It gives you the power to use that achievement for your own gain. In essence, celebration makes you powerful as a person. You can stand tall amid the crowd because of your new rank. People can look up to you and admire you because of your being powerful is attractive.

(c) Celebration helps you to savour the moment of your achievement.

When you savour something, you are fully aware of the pleasure you derive from it. Thus, celebration helps you in being conscious of the pleasure you derive from the arrival of your newly delivered dream. The savouring of that pleasant moment is the result of your paying deliberate, conscious attention to it. You are being mindful of it and this goes a long way in creating a mental picture that can be stored in your brain.

(d) Celebration helps you create memories.

In addition to creating mental pictures when savouring your moment of joy, celebration also helps you create physical memories. When you have photographs taken of the event, you are storing up physical items that you can refer to in the future. If you receive accolades during your celebration, audio recordings of these could serve as memory stores that you can tap into when you need them.

CELEBRATING THE WAY YOU DESIRE

Just as other aspects of your dream journey, when you decide to celebrate your newly realized goal, it is up to you to choose how. In essence, you have the right to celebrate in the way that you desire.

Celebrations do not always imply huge gatherings or big spending. A simple gathering of your close associates in a place you can afford will serve an equal purpose to a much grander event. It is a matter of mindset. Moreover, you have the right to celebrate your various dream achievements in different ways. It all depends on the value and meaning you attach to the particular dream you are commemorating.

Your strength to celebrate may be challenged by people who have opposite opinions about your feat. Some may feel that the feat you have performed is not necessary. To them, your new status is not meaningful. Others may feel that you, in particular, should not have been capable of performing the feat. The negative opinions of others may be expressed out of sheer jealousy. They may silently wish that they were the ones to have accomplished what is now yours.

Whatever the negative opinions, you should be aware that they do not count. Recognize that these opposing opinions do not reflect your own opinion as regards this new dream you have birthed. And as far as relevancy goes, it is your opinion that matters. Call to mind the fact that the wildness of your dreams had always been yours right from conception. And it is yours even at the time of celebration. Do not allow someone to rain on your parade. Go for your celebration the way you intend to have it done.

While celebrating the way you want, however, remember to be cognizant of the needs of those around you. In addition, be aware of the fact that the celebration is not just about you. If you have effectively carried other people along with you in your journey towards attaining this goal, they too, should be celebrating.

REMEMBERING THOSE WHO HELPED YOU ALONG THE WAY

An essential aspect of celebration is acknowledging the people who helped you reach the height you have recently attained. In Chapter 8, I mentioned that sometimes, during the process of protruding your dream, you may have stepped on some toes. Your extreme growth might have required you to take some space or time that belonged to some people in your circle of influence. Maybe you got some other people to do what you would normally do so that you could allocate some resources towards achieving your dream. Now that your dream has been realized, it is wise to acknowledge those people who endured a bit of discomfort on your journey to realize your new dream.

Apart from this group of people, you also need to acknowledge other individuals that helped you at various stages of your journey. Maybe the revival of your dream was as a result of a stimulus you received from some associate or family member. It would be indicated to mention this influence on the vital course of action of your dream journey. Perhaps, without them, you would not have had the strength to start all over again in the first place.

Also, if you used the assistance of some folks during conception, growth or birthing of your dream, it is sensible to offer such people some recognition during your celebrations.

Having established these aspects of celebrations, let us consider what happens when various prevailing factors cause someone not to have the strength to celebrate. What happens when an individual is not allowed to celebrate their achievement?

DEPRIVED OF THE OPPORTUNITY TO CELEBRATE

Giving birth to a dream is meant to be joyous, empowering and pleasurable. And so is the ability to celebrate your accomplishment. When an individual is restricted from celebrating their hard-earned achievement, a significant part of his/her joy and victory is being taken away from him or her. In turn, this means that they may not be fulfilled despite the fact that they have achieved their goal. Consider the following cases when some individuals' strength to celebrate waned even after great successes:

- A teenager had secretly studied for a particular course against his parents' advice. He studied music in a situation where his parents favoured sports over music. When he finished and passed the final exam, he found it difficult to share his joy with his family. The environment was not conducive to celebrating his newly delivered dream. He did not trust the people he loved to give him the recognition he desired at a critical point of his life.

- A young woman married the love of her life against her parents' wish. She had gotten engaged to someone of a different faith, belief and practice. Her parents would have rather seen her married to someone of their own faith and beliefs. They refused to attend her wedding. To this young woman, the celebration of her wedding should be a real moment of joy. However, the issue with her parents sapped her strength to celebrate to a significant extent on a very memorable day of her life.

- A business man had worked hard to re-launch his golfing enterprise. He had failed at his first attempt at the sporting business. When he revived his dream, he worked hard and with determination, managed to gather enough resources to start again. He also employed the services of a business coach to guide and support him through the process. He totally revamped the system, acquired new technology and tapped into a growing niche of golfing in his environment. In fact by the second year of his re-launching, his books were back in the black. He was generating much more income than he ever had all through his married life. He decided to celebrate the upturn of his business. However, his wife was not going to have any of it. She maintained that he needed to have five times as much revenue before he could have any form of celebration. Subconsciously, she was using her rebellion as a 'compensation' for the difficult years in between when the family had to live on minimal financial resources. The wife's unhealthy attitude about the past impacted negatively on her husband's strength to celebrate.

- An athletic young man had the dream of growing his muscles to an enormous extent from an early age. He just loved a muscular body and always wished to have one. He had even idolized someone with such a body and always admired this fellow. So, as a young adult, as soon as he had a steady job, he employed the service of a personal trainer. He was all out to work towards his dream. He invested in the right equipment and even signed up for regular delivery of nutritional materials. After a full year of this regimen, the young man acquired the type of muscle-built that he had dreamed of. He was very proud of himself and decided to celebrate. However, he could not identify any one in his family who would buy into the idea of celebrating this kind of achievement. His family members felt muscle building was a wild dream. A perception of not being able to have a real celebration with those he loved was worrisome to the young man. That fact sapped him of his strength to celebrate to some extent.

The examples cited above show that the strength to celebrate should not be taken for granted. Being able to celebrate your new dream achievements is an important part of your fulfillment in life.

Having established the relevancy of the strength to celebrate, the questions are:

> *Are you actually engaging your strength to celebrate maximally as you birth new dreams? Are you taking full advantage of the premium of celebration towards your fulfillment in life?*

YOUR PAST CELEBRATIONS OF DREAM ACHIEVEMENTS

The next set of exercises will help you towards using celebrations to fully appreciate your dream achievement. They will help you identify things that may be preventing you from savouring your moment of glory.

Using the previous insights in this chapter, let us take a quick look at your life. In Chapter 3, you created a life line that described key events in your past life. You made a list of your past dream achievements such as marriage, graduation, purchase of a car and so on. Try and re-collect how you celebrated at least two of the events you listed. In the space below, write down your recollection.

_____

_____

_____

_____

_____

• STRENGTH TO CELEBRATE •

Now take another look at your life line. Are there any accomplishments that you did not celebrate?

If yes, write those achievements down in the space below.

For the items in the last list, list any reasons for which you did not have a celebration to mark those achievements.

In addition to the above, ask yourself some pertinent questions:
- When was your celebration the highest point of your dream achievement journey?
- When was your strength to celebrate taken away from you?

- How did you feel when you were able to celebrate your achievements?
- How did you feel when you were not allowed to celebrate or when people were not supportive of your celebration?

Take a stab at answering the questions honestly. Maybe you were able to recollect an unpleasant period of your life that was a result of your inability to celebrate properly.

To help you reconnect with the present, ask yourself the following questions:

In your present circumstances, if you were to celebrate one or more of those events for which you didn't have the chance to celebrate in the past, what would you do? How would you celebrate such an event today in your present circumstances?

_____
_____
_____
_____
_____
_____

The honest inquiry is to ask yourself: If the circumstances were in favour of my celebrating any of these accomplishments, would I, actually, take time to celebrate properly? Am I taking time to enjoy the moments of my achievement?

• STRENGTH TO CELEBRATE •

LEARNING TO SAVOUR IS ESSENTIAL TO HAPPINESS

The last exercise might have helped you to identify some deep truths. A celebration is a means of savouring your accomplishment. However, celebration is only one way of savouring your moment of glory. Taking time to stay in the present and actually enjoy moments of your achievement may require more mindfulness from you. You may also savour your accomplishment by having talks about it or finding other means of sharing it with others. You may create a slide show of photographs taken during the progression of your dream as well as the celebrations you had when you realized it. You may decide to invite friends and family over just to share these memories and your experience. If you are creative, you may go to the extent of writing a song or poem about your achievement.

All these different methods of deliberately and consciously paying attention to the moment of your dream's fulfillment will add up towards your true happiness. The additional effort you invest into taking pleasure in your moment of accomplishment goes a long way to enhance your fulfillment in general. In addition, savouring your moment of achievement at an appropriate time and in appropriate manners makes you whole as a person. When you are able to acknowledge the moment and create enough mental and physical memories, you will not be attached to that moment and live only through it. You are able to move on from that moment to accomplish newer dreams and attain greater accomplishments.

When it comes to celebrating old and new achievements, there is no age limit. Age is no barrier to acquiring the strength to celebrate over and over again. Jenny Wood Allen can testify to that fact.

ACQUIRING THE STRENGTH TO CELEBRATE HAS NO AGE LIMIT

Jenny Wood-Allen from Dundee, Scotland, was 87 years old when she completed the 1999 London Marathon with a time of 7hrs. 14min. 46sec. The London Marathon is 26 miles, 385 yards! This achievement placed her in the Guinness Book of World Record for being the Oldest Female Marathon Finisher.

Jenny's story (1-2) is unique and interesting. As a child, she never enjoyed athletics and always came last in race meets. However, in her youth, she took up other sports and became a Scottish cycling champion as a time triallist in the 1930s. And then, at age 71, Jenny took up marathon running for the first time. This was after a 40 year break from sports! That was a long period of interruption.

Jenny's stimulus to revive her sports' dream came as a result of her desire to raise money for cancer charities. With this motivation, Jenny re-launched her dream into the world of marathon running. She faced initial opposition due to her age. Her doctor advised her that even though she had the lung capacity of someone half her age, she should not go in for marathon races. He even predicted that it would take her around nine hours to finish the race. However, Jenny believed she could do it, and clocked 5 hours and 34 minutes in that first come-back marathon.

Jenny indeed had strength to bring forth her dream even at the age of 71. In addition to being one of the top five international marathons, the London Marathon is a huge celebratory sporting event. It is also one of the World Marathon Majors being in the same league as the Boston, Chicago, New York and Berlin Marathons. This international standard of the race afforded Jenny the opportunity to celebrate in many different ways and with dynamic populations of people.

Since her first success, Jenny has run in up to 30 different marathons. Therefore, she has multiplied her strength to celebrate many times over. She ran in the London Marathon 16 times and has taken part in the New York Marathon. She has raised some 40,000 Pounds Sterling for charity.

In 1990, Jenny, then aged 90 years and 145 days, completed the London Marathon again in 11 hours 34 minutes. This was Jenny's last participation in marathon races. She retired from big events after that occasion. However, Jenny still takes part in occasional walks.

Jenny took her love for the race even further. She set up the Tayside, Scotland branch of the Running Sisters—a group of women of all ages who run for friendship, fitness and fun.

MULTIPLYING THE STRENGTH TO CELEBRATE

Jenny continues to have more strength to celebrate as she receives nominations from different bodies honouring her lifetime achievements. In 2001, Jenny's strength to bring forth was celebrated at the London's Savoy Hotel. She received the Help the Aged NOJO (Not Old Just Older) Award for outstanding sporting achievement (2). In 2005 she was one of six semi-finalists of the 2005 Scotswoman of the year (3).

Jenny Wood Allen did not let her age inhibit the revival of a dream. Neither did she let the long hiatus she had taken from active sports hinder her. She believed she could do it despite oppositions from key players in her life. She worked hard towards attaining her goal, motivated by her desire to make a difference in the lives of people through money raised for cancer charities. Jenny Wood Allen has demonstrated an outstanding strength to deliver that which could not be limited by age!

Jenny's strength to celebrate continues to be demonstrated after she has retired from active participation in marathons. She is involved with her community sports and continues to inspire people of all generations. In addition, a number of sporting awards are being given in the name of Jenny Wood Allen. Thus, Jenny's strength to celebrate is continually being passed on in various dimensions!

Having the strength to celebrate is a lively aspect of the dream achievement process. But as important as celebration is, it is only one aspect of the post-achievement themes. Taking ownership of your newly delivered dream requires other actions apart from celebrations.

WHAT DOES IT MEAN TO TAKE OWNERSHIP?

Taking ownership of your newly delivered dream means that you are taking full responsibility over all matters that result from your achievement. When you take ownership, you are acknowledging that you are in charge. You are the owner and you are declaring the fact to the world around you. You engage yourself in the outcome of the accomplishment. When it comes to taking the glory for your hard work, you are there. That honour for the effort invested belongs to you. No one else should take it away from you by any means whatsoever. That was one of the themes around your celebrations. In addition, since the end-result of this dream is yours, you're not the only one who has to acknowledge its ownership. It goes beyond peripheral knowledge. Taking ownership means you have to act like you are the owner.

You have to take over the control of any responsibilities associated with your newly delivered dream. If there are things to settle, you settle them or delegate the tying of loose ends to someone else. If there are any complaints or grievances associated with this new achievement, you stand and face them. You have to defend your rights to enjoy and claim this new achievement as yours if you come under any attack. At times, taking ownership may require you to prove beyond all doubt that your new dream is an achievement of yours that has come to stay. Or you may need to affirm that this new accomplishment of yours is a star that you have earned on your flag and no one is going to take it away from you.

The following is the story of one man who had to carry out this affirmation step of taking ownership of his dream. He had to demonstrate beyond all doubt that his newly delivered dream at that time was actually his to keep.

TEACHING RUNS IN JAIME'S FAMILY

Jaime Escalante had a teacher's blood running in his veins (4). Born to a double teacher parent lineage in Bolivia, Jaime went on to become a teacher. It was a classic 'it runs in the family' story. Escalante taught in his home country for 12 years. Then he got the hitch to find a better life in the United States. He relocated from Puerto Rico to California in 1964. With this move came an interruption in Jaime's teaching career. In this period of interruption, Jaime had to tackle a number of challenges. He had to learn to speak English and obtain the teaching certification of the United States.

In fact, he had to earn another college degree in electronics first. To sustain himself financially during this break, Jaime took on many odd jobs.

After obtaining the college degree, Jaime took a day job in a computer software corporation. He continued his schooling at night to earn a Bachelor of Arts in Mathematics. He then went on to obtain his long-desired teaching credentials. It just seemed he could not get teaching out of his veins. After obtaining his teaching certificate and BA in math, he revived the dream of his original career. He applied to the School Board and got posted to Garfield High School in East Los Angeles in 1974.

A VISION FOR MAKING A DIFFERENCE IN THE LIVES OF STUDENTS

With his teaching dream revived, Escalante went all out to make a difference in the lives of young folks. However, the situation he met at Garfield was even more challenging than he envisaged. The school was known for violence and drugs and the students were troubled. In fact, some other teachers had dismissed the students as 'un-teachable'. At first, Garfield wanted to turn back. He called his former employer at the computer company to ask for his old job back.

However, Escalante decided to stay on when he found twelve students willing to take an algebra class.

Escalante had a great vision that helped him conquer his circumstances. He saw beneath the rough surface of these students and saw their potential. He therefore strove to help draw out this potential and make them the best they could be.

• STRENGTH TO CELEBRATE •

A UNIQUE ACHIEVEMENT

In 1979, Escalante started teaching his first calculus class—a challenge no other teacher wanted. He thought this approach would help improve lower level mathematics' course. Escalante devised different means of communicating the subject to the students and eventually won their confidence and listening attention. He prepared them for the Advanced Placement (A.P.) calculus administered by the Educational Testing Service (ETS).

Jaime's strength to deliver in teaching was brought under the national spotlight in 1982. This was the year when every one of the 18 students in his class passed the AP calculus exam. This was a unique achievement, considering the background level at which these students were when Jaime first started with them.

NO STRENGTH TO CELEBRATE

In the moment of rejoicing over this unusual accomplishment and celebrating his newly delivered dream, Jaime's strength to celebrate was challenged. The ETS queried the scores of the students and questioned the validity of the test procedure. It was rumoured that the students cheated and had obtained the exam questions prior to the test date.

Both Escalante and his students were crushed. This was their hard-earned dream being taken away from them. Jaime decided to defend all rights to this dream. He protested and argued that his students were disqualified because of a wrong perception of their ability; they were of Hispanic background and from a poor school. In a bid to prove the testing body wrong, 14 students agreed to re-take the test under the scrutiny of the local highest officials of the body. All of the students passed the test the second time around. They had a greater cause to celebrate.

TAKING OWNERSHIP OF A DREAM ACHIEVEMENT

When their first success was challenged, Jaime and his students found that they had to take ownership of their newly delivered dream. They had to *reserve all rights* to their great exam scores. They had to stand firm, not allowing someone to quash their newly acquired strength to celebrate.

Taking a stand to defend all rights to his dream and that of his students on that first occasion has resulted in even greater dream achievements for Jaime. His strength to deliver and celebrate continued to multiply after the events of 1982. He not only re-claimed his first success, he also became empowered for more action. And the fact that he was able to stand tall in the face of his accomplishment attracted more people to him. More students enrolled in Jaime's class the following year. In addition, he got more support from the school administration immediately after that contested victory. By 1987, the number of students in Jaime's program that passed the AP calculus exam had risen to 73. By 1991, the number of students who took the advanced placement examinations in mathematics and other subjects had escalated to 570!

STRENGTH TO CELEBRATE IN CELEBRITY CIRCLES

Escalante's strength to deliver became better known in national circles, when, in 1988, his classroom challenges and successes were the subject of a book release entitled: '*Jaime Escalante: The Best Teacher in America*'. Also, in 1988 Warner Bros. released a movie called *Stand*

and Deliver (5), the story of Escalante's dedication to excellence in teaching. It illustrated how Jaime worked against all odds and was able to transform underachieving Latino students into high achievers who scored high grades in their Advanced Placement calculus exams.

In addition, Jaime's celebrity status became even better established when he became the host of an instructional television series on the Public Broadcasting Service (PBS). The program entitled *Futures* introduces students to a variety of mathematics and science-based careers. It is a popular classroom program in the history of PBS which has received over 50 awards from professional and educational organizations.

Escalante has also received many awards for his contributions to the field of education. These include honorary doctorate awards from five universities across the United States. He was also awarded the Presidential Medal for Excellence by former President Ronald Reagan in 1988. In 1999, Jaime was inducted into the National Teachers' Hall of Fame. Thus, Escalante had many more diversified opportunities to celebrate his achievements. Taking ownership of his accomplishment when he needed to broadened the horizon of his strength to celebrate.

Escalante indeed had the strength to deliver his life's mission as a teacher, and made a significant difference in the lives of many students. Escalante had the strength to nurture his newly delivered dream in 1982. That nurturing yielded a higher enrolment in his classes, resulting in more classes of successful students over the course of the next 10 years. He influenced students not only at Garfield but also in the Sacramento, California School District where he took up an appointment at a later time in his career.

While delivering his life's mission, Jaime has demonstrated the strength to multiply his first dream many times over. This has resulted in even more strength to celebrate as he received many awards from both state and national bodies.

Today Escalante's students have become well-established career professionals making differences in the lives of people all over the globe. These students can testify that Jaime did influence them to acquire the strength to deliver their life's mission (6).

SHARING IN OTHER PEOPLES' CELEBRATIONS

Earlier in this chapter, I mentioned that some new dream achievers may find it challenging to get the support of other people when it comes to celebrating their success. Often, this may be because these people did not support the dream goal in the first place. However, the reason for the lack of support for a celebrating individual may be due to a factor in that individual himself. It could be that the new dream achiever did not carry other people along with him when he was pursuing his dream. On the other hand, the dream achiever may be someone who actually does not support other people in their own celebrations.

It is essential that you acknowledge other people's achievements and celebrate with them in appropriate ways during their occasions of joy. Having a perception that other people have a right to their dreams and celebrating their successes the way they desire is a right attitude to life. This attitude will free you to acquire the strength to celebrate when it is your turn to acknowledge a new achievement. When you celebrate with others, they will more likely support you in your own celebrations.

• STRENGTH TO CELEBRATE •

A celebration is one of the high points of your dream achievement journey. Celebrating your accomplishment is part of carrying the memories forward. It builds you up for future dreams. Savouring the moment of your achievement helps you stop in time and deliberately acknowledge your new status. This helps you move forward with more enthusiasm from that point forward. It imparts in you the strength to conceive more dreams, work towards them and bring them forth. Having the strength to celebrate is empowering.

Celebrations and savouring the moment of your achievement are essential elements to taking ownership of your dream. However, in order to take full ownership of your dream, you have to take on full responsibility for the end result of your achievement. Taking ownership may require you to stand up and defend your dream if necessary.

Taking ownership of your dream by taking on full responsibility is fundamental. The responsibility for your dream involves providing for and nurturing it. That is the subject of the next chapter.

CHAPTER 11

Strength to Provide

Nurturing your newly delivered dream

In the last chapter, I discussed celebrations as a means of taking ownership of your newly delivered dream. I also highlighted the fact that celebration is one of many actions you need to take to ensure continued ownership of the new position you have as a result of your recent dream achievement. Most of the other action steps you have to take towards safeguarding ownership of your new dream revolve around the ability to nurture and provide for it.

Having the strength to provide is an important element of sustaining the existence of your new dream. Nurturing your dream is essentially having an attitude of maintenance towards the new status you acquired during your recent dream achievement.

NURTURING AS A WAY OF LIFE

Nurturing is a way of propagating life. For any living object to survive, it has to obtain nourishment from some sources. Using the childbirth imagery, when a baby is born, one of the first set of actions performed by the mother is breastfeeding. In fact, the first milk that is released during breastfeeding is useful in passing some immunity to the baby. It is essential that the mother is able to nourish the baby on a regular basis as the growth and survival of the baby depend on it.

Although feeding is essential to the nurturing of a newborn, it is only one aspect of it. Nurturing also involves all forms of care of the baby. That means supplying all of the necessary items required for his day to day living. When you nurture a living object, you are in essence looking after it. You are cultivating it so that it grows. Nurturing does necessarily involve cherishing. It is easier to provide for someone you cherish. In a similar manner, when you cherish someone, you take steps to ensure that their needs are met.

PROVIDING FOR YOUR NEW DREAM IS A VITAL PART OF OWNERSHIP

Taking ownership of your new dream begins when you recognize that its continued existence depends on the decisions, efforts and actions *you* take and not on those taken by someone else. This recognition should spur you on to make a commitment to the process that will propagate your new status. In many cases, this process is one of maintenance, which is essentially a furthering of the goals you had when you were still growing the dream. Maintaining your newly delivered dream means you will divert some of your resources towards its continued and flourishing existence. Such resources include time, finances, intellectual efforts and physical resources. Nurturing your new dream will also involve cherishing it. That means standing up for it and protecting it from any attacks. Cherishing your dream means not neglecting it but paying attention to it. Nurturing your dream may require you to continue sharing the fact of its existence so that other people will get to know of its reality.

MATCHING THE DREAM WITH THE RIGHT TYPE OF RESOURCES

Taking care of different categories of dreams will require the supply of a different combination of various resources. For instance, providing for a newly delivered relationship dream will require a significant amount of your time and personal effort. For someone who newly delivered a marriage dream by going to the altar with his/her loved one, cherishing that dream will mean cherishing his/her new life-partner. Providing for this dream requires a significant input of one-on-one time together. This is an effort that cannot be delegated to someone else. Compared to any other resources that may be required, your own, personal input is a priority.

Nurturing a newly delivered business dream will also involve a lot of time input, but of a different kind. For a business dream, the time input required does not have to be spent solely with one person. It may be with different individuals in a way that results in an enormous total amount of time when summed up. In addition to the time input, a business dream may require a significant amount of financial resources towards publicity. If you have just delivered a business dream, you will need to nurture that new creation of yours and give it wings to fly as you let others know about it. This is essential if the business is to survive and be profitable.

INTEGRATING YOUR NEW DREAM INTO YOUR ENVIRONMENT

Taking ownership of your newly delivered dream also involves integrating it into the existing structure of your family and/or career. Integration is the act of mixing or incorporating. It may involve the combination or the addition of two or more materials. On the other hand, it could involve gradually replacing an old item with a new one in a way that will not jeopardize the already existing structure.

When you integrate your new dream into your way of life, you are taking ownership of it. You are ensuring that the dream is also cherished by people in your circle of influence. If someone has any issues about it, you need to talk with them so that they can review their stand gradually (not forcefully). You need to continue to let such fellows know that your dream has come to stay and that it is essential for them to welcome it into the environment where it is supposed to subsist.

Integrating your dream into your environment may require you to take some lessons from your experience while your dream was still in gestation.

DRAWING A CUE FROM YOUR PERIODIC EVALUATIONS

In Chapters 7 and 8, I highlighted the value of periodic evaluations during the growth and protrusion phases of your dream. I discussed the need to change tactics as necessary if you sensed that some factors in your environment were presenting some form of opposition to the growth of your dream. In a similar way, you might have found that some factors really helped push your dream along faster during its growth phase. Now that you have been able to bring forth your dream, you need to take forward the lessons you learnt from your experience of growing the dream. Taking ownership of your dream will require you to use those insights to your advantage towards integrating your dream into your circumstances or lifestyle.

Make efforts to ensure that any factors, which presented threats to the process of your goals' realization are not re-introduced. In some cases, such factors no longer exist and you may not have to worry about them. On the other hand, it is possible that such adverse factors are still menacingly present after your dream delivery. You might have been able to negotiate your way around them during the growth phase, but they never ceased to exist. This fact may imply that your newly delivered dream is still at risk from such hostile factors. Taking ownership of your dream requires you to find means of ensuring that those factors will not harm your new-born dream in any way. This may involve building walls of resistance to form barriers or shields against such invasive factors.

On the other hand, if you recognize that some factors, which helped in the growth of your dream, are still in place, feel free to take advantage of them. Use such positive factors to continue to propagate and promote your dream. A word of caution here; you should ascertain that such factors have not changed since you have delivered the dream. Confirm that, in your new circumstances, such factors are still going to work towards the development of your dream and not against it.

Having the strength to provide for a newly delivered dream is an excellent premise on which to maintain and build upon the status you have recently attained. However, for some individuals, the actual dream they desire to bring forth in the first place is that of the capacity to provide for their basic human needs. Such was the premise behind Legson Kayira's dream.

BRIDGING THE GAP BETWEEN POVERTY AND PROSPERITY

For Legson Kayira, distance was no barrier when it came to having strength to bring forth his vision of an ideal future. Legson's dream was highly desirable. It required him to bridge an intellectual gap between poverty and prosperity. However, to close this gap, Kayira had to cross a big gulf of land and sea. This huge physical gap separated the place where he was and the place of his vision of an ideal future. What was extraordinary about Legson's story is the strategy he planned to employ to bridge that huge gap. His goal was to cross the land portion of the distance—3200kms.—on foot! As to the sea portion of the chasm separating him from his ultimate destination, Legson had little idea of how he was going to close the gap when he set off on his journey. However, Legson had a solid conviction that the combined distance of land and sea he had to cover was surmountable as he held on tight to his unimaginable dream.

The broad theme of Legson's all-encompassing dream was that of serving mankind and making a difference in the world. Born in 1942 in Nyasaland (now Malawi), Africa, to poor and illiterate parents, Legson's first exposure to the world of education came as a result of contact with Scottish missionaries. He had to travel about three miles to get to his first school. It took his parents many months to pay the year's meagre tuition of that time. Legson eventually went to junior high school and applied to teacher's college. His application did not go through because he was too young. His only other option for continuing his education was to attend a secondary school, which was 200 miles away from his village. By this time, his father had died and his mother felt it was wrong for him to pursue his education. He was much needed in making a living to provide for his family.

CHALLENGING THE STATUS QUO

Legson, however, saw his education as a way out of poverty. He recognized that in order to be able to get over and beyond poverty level, he had to obtain a higher level of education than what was traditionally offered in his village. So, he continued into secondary school and completed his graduation requirements. Upon graduation, Legson reached another crossroad in his life. He had the choice of following the traditional route in his land at that time. That route was to attend teachers college and then take up a job locally as a teacher. It was an easy route and his family had expected him to follow it. However, Kayira could not be confined by culture or tradition. He had conceived a vision of an ideal future that was bigger than tradition. That vision comprised the unimaginable concept of going to America to obtain a college education. Legson believed so much in his dream that he began sharing it with his family after his secondary education. He started challenging the status quo. No one in his village had ever earned a degree from an American college. Kayira went on to announce to his village that he was going to walk to America on a set date. His plan was to walk from his tribal village in Nyasaland (Southeastern Africa) north across Cairo (North Africa) where he would board a ship to America!

HOW FAR CAN A MAN TRAVEL ON FOOT TO CATCH HIS DREAM?

Kayira set out on his journey at age 17. All he had for his journey was a small axe for protection, a blanket, enough food for 5 days, a map of Africa and two books—the Bible and John Bunyan's *Pilgrim's Progress*. He was barefoot and penniless. His illiterate family had no idea where America was, but reluctantly gave him their blessings.

Legson walked through the wet and dry seasons, storms and jungles and did odd jobs along the way until he got to Mwanza on Lake Victoria (Tanzania, East Africa). There, he had to interrupt his journey as he worked for six months to earn enough money for a trip to Kampala, in Uganda (East Africa). After more than a year from the date he started out, Kayira got to Kampala. While working in Uganda, Legson had the opportunity to find a library that had a directory of American Colleges. The first entry he found was that of Skagit College in Mount Vernon, Washington. Legson wrote to this college and was offered admission with a full scholarship and assistance towards finding a job in the States!

Legson saw his dream gradually taking shape. However, he had to wait in Kampala until the following August when he finally got a Nyasaland passport and a visa to enter Sudan (North Africa). After another long journey on foot and hitch-hiking, Legson got to Sudan where he applied for the United States Visa. At this point, Legson faced another interruption as he had no money for the journey from Sudan to America. However, Kayira received aid from his would-be-school colleagues. The Skagit Valley students and the Mount Vernon Community raised the money to bring Kayira to Washington State. Thus, over 2 years after he began his journey, Legson set foot in an American college to obtain an American degree! That was an enormous accomplishment for Legson. He defied all barriers, obstacles, interruptions that prevented him from birthing his dream.

THE STRENGTH TO PROVIDE FOR AN EDUCATION DREAM

With all the attention that his story got, Kayira became a minor celebrity when he finally got to Mount Vernon. His determination and sense of purpose towards his education goal had attracted much attention. He was in demand as a public speaker in many circles. He had to turn down many requests, though, because of his commitments as a full-time student. During his first summer in the United States, Kayira went on speaking tours and was able to save money from the honoraria towards his education. Hence, in the short term, Legson had the strength to provide for his newly delivered dream at that time.

Kayira subsequently attended the University of Washington after his Skagit College education and obtained a B.A. in Political Science in 1965. However, he did not stop at this level of education. He attended St. Catherine's College of the University of Cambridge, England and became a professor of political Science in the same institution. Legson became a widely respected author, his first book being his autobiography (1).

Legson Kayira's dream was his life's mission. According to the letter he sent to Skagit Valley, his journey was 'to glory or death' (2). When he set out to accomplish the unimaginable, his dream was broad based—to get an American education. However, as he set forth to accomplish one goal after the other, it became increasingly clear what kind of steps he needed to take. He gradually got clarity on which college he was to attend and what it took for him to travel to the United States. His faith and determination were instrumental to finding the strength he needed to grow, and bring forth the initial and subsequent dreams.

MULTIPLYING THE STRENGTH TO PROVIDE

Legson Kayira got an American college education and found his way out of poverty. Bringing forth that dream has equipped him to fulfill the dream of financial independence. His ability to bring forth his dream was the result of the positive mindset which he developed right from the time he conceived his vision of an ideal future. The ideal future he had envisioned was one in which he lived without poverty. It was one in which he had the strength to provide for his material and physical needs as he attained financial independence. Legson had put himself in the driver's seat, taking ownership of the responsibility to make that ideal future real. He knew that for his dream to be realized, he had to make the decisions and carry out the actions towards making it happen. As he later affirmed in his autobiography:

> *"I learned I was not, as most Africans believed, the victim of my circumstances but the master of them."*(1)

Kayira's strength to provide has been multiplied many times over since his first major dream achievement. He has had the strength to bring forth other dreams with bigger goals as he obtained degrees higher than the original Bachelors that he first pursued. As he launched into an academic career, his strength to provide was increasingly manifested. Legson Kayira keeps on finding the strength to provide for the other dreams he continues to bring forth.

• STRENGTH TO PROVIDE •

As I discussed in Chapter 2, realizing some goals can help meet various human needs. Many dreams are born out of the desire to fill a void that exists in one's life or circumstances. When such a dream is fulfilled, it gives the individual a new strength to launch forth many new goals.

Ruth Munce Hill captured her vision of an ideal future which rose from a great human need she had.

A DREAM ARISING OUT OF A PERSONAL NEED

For Ruth Munce Hill, having a Christian education was on top of her priority list for her children. However, during her time, there was a void for such in her community.

Ruth had just recently lost both her husband and her mother. She was at a crossroads in life. She relocated to Tampa Bay, Florida with her two sons where she took up a job at St. Petersburg High School, teaching Bible history. However, that did not last very long as the School Board decided to drop the subject from their curriculum. That was another life-changing event for Ruth. It was then that she decided to revive her interrupted dream of college education, which she had previously started at Wheaton College but was interrupted by World War I. Ruth was successful during this attempt and she got her teacher's certificate.

At this point, Ruth's wish for her sons came alive. Desiring a Christian education for them, but finding none in her locality, Hill's instincts were stimulated. She dreamt of setting up a Christian school of her own. Her vision of an ideal future for her sons served as a need waiting to be fulfilled. So, in the fall of 1952, Ruth founded a new Christian school with the help of her friends (3). Through this means she brought forth her dream of Christian education for her sons. In addition, something bigger had been put in place through the achievement of Ruth's dream. Many other parents who wanted a Christian education for their kids found a suitable school that offered this.

Thus Ruth's original dream for education grew into a public service one. Ruth remained principal of the school for at least ten years and she taught Bible and English classes. Thus, Ruth's own desire for a career position was also fulfilled. Subsequently, Ruth handed over management of the school to Bill Caldwell who was affiliated with Keswick Radio stations and the Southern Keswick Bible Conference. In 1962 the school was renamed Keswick Christian School.

PROVIDING FOR A NEWLY DELIVERED DREAM

An interesting part of Ruth's story was how she found the strength to provide for her dream when it was newly delivered. Running a privately-owned school definitely required a huge amount of funding. As Ruth was both widowed and orphaned, she had to find a means of providing for the dream to which she had given birth. Here is how she did it.

Ruth's mother, Grace Livingston Hill had died in the midst of writing a novel. Grace's publishers asked Ruth to finish her mother's book, and she took on that challenge. She successfully delivered this dream. The strength she acquired from this achievement served as a stimulus for her to write her own books. She published a total of six Christian romances. Ruth poured the revenue she received from her writing into financing the school she had founded. Therefore, through her hard work, strength and creativity, Hill was equipped with the strength to provide financially for her dream.

A SHORT TERM PROVISION LED TO A LEGACY

For Ruth, taking care of her newly delivered dream resulted in more strength to celebrate for many years afterwards. Even though she had passed on the leadership of the school to other hands, the fact remains that, without her initial provision and nurture, the school she founded would never have grown enough to attract new investors. Because she acquired the strength to provide in the short term, immediately after launching the school, the administrators, who took over from her, had even greater strength to provide for the long term.

Ruth lived to see her 103rd birthday in 2001. She celebrated with Keswick students in her residence at Pinecrest Place, Largo, Pinellas County, Florida. She enjoyed celebrating with the students as they demonstrated the greatness of her legacy. They witnessed to the fact that Ruth indeed had the strength to bring forth her dream, provide for it and see it multiply for up to 50 years after the original dream was realized.

Both Legson Kayira and Ruth Munce Hill had the strength to provide for their dreams in the short term. On the long term, Legson had the strength to provide for his dream through the academic career that he pursued after his education. In Ruth's case, her strength to provide in the short term also resulted in a continuing strength to provide for the legacy she left behind through the Keswick Christian School.

OVERCOMING OPPOSITIONS TO NURTURING

As nurturing is essential to the growth and propagation of your newly delivered dream, it is essential that you overcome any opposition that present a threat to your ability to acquiring the strength to provide.

There are a number of factors that could sap you of the strength to provide. These include:
- Fear and emotional stress
- Taking on another big dream pursuit too soon
- Lack of relevant information about nurture
- Fatigue

(a) Overcoming fear and emotional stress:

Fear of the unknown is a factor that is present at almost every stage of your dream growth. When you have given birth to the dream, the fear factor may also show up again. To overcome fear, you need to keep re-affirming your capacity. You need to re-assure yourself that you have been capable of doing all of the hard work required to bring your dream up to the delivery point and past it. You need to build confidence in your ability to provide for this dream just as you have been able to carry out the previous steps.

If you are having any emotional stress after your dream delivery, you need to beat the post-partum blues. Just like mothers who experience sadness after childbirth, you need to tap into emotional support of friends and family to overcome the challenges of the period.

(b) Taking rest between dream conceptions:

During the period after the delivery of your new dream, it is essential not to begin work on a new vision or concept that may be demanding in terms of allocation of resources. Take time to focus on nurturing your new dream for a given period. Do not rush to take on a new, similarly demanding dream project. This will help you ensure that you have enough stamina and physical energy for the process of supplying what your already delivered dream requires for its survival.

(c) Keep on getting relevant information:

The way to overcome lack of information or adequate knowledge about any process is straightforward. Employ the resources within your reach to get the information required regarding the ways of nurturing the dream to which you have given birth. Having the appropriate and relevant information will work well in your decision-making process.

(d) Getting rid of fatigue:

Fatigue may occur during the nurturing period of your dream because you have focused on only one project for a very long period of time. When you have resumed your normal duties after the first period of rest post-delivery, always ensure that you take regular breaks while nurturing your newly delivered dream. Use a variety of avenues of relaxation during those breaks. When you engage in different activities that provide varying stimulation of interest, your focus is sharpened when you get back to the action steps of nurturing your dream.

PROPAGATING GOOD HEALTH

The health and fitness industry thrives on helping people to achieve and maintain 'wellness'. But, without the individual's active participation, the great amount of resources available will be meaningless. Each of us needs to take responsibility for our health. This is even more important in the period following recovery from illness. In order to continue enjoying the new status of good health you have just assumed, you need to nurture it. Maintaining that good health you have obtained is the theme behind taking ownership of it. You need to provide for your newly delivered dream of good health by cultivating it and taking actions towards its growth. Taking care of your good health is a step towards ensuring that it does not die. It is a means of affirming that you do not return to poor health again.

Mavis Lindgren is one woman whose life's mission was directed to maintaining the good health she attained after a period of illness.

BRINGING FORTH A DREAM OF GOOD HEALTH

As a registered nurse, Mavis Lindgren was well informed about what it takes to get over an illness as well as maintaining a healthy lifestyle. She was also aware that her overall health had not always been the greatest. Before she ever got into training as a nurse, she had been a 'victim' of awful childhood illnesses. Mavis had attacks of whooping cough and pneumonia at two years of age in a very cold community of rural Manitoba in Canada. As a teenager she had a slight case of tuberculosis. She was plagued by chronic chest colds, which frequently turned into pneumonia as she grew older. In addition, in her adult years she suffered from arthritis.

When, in her early retirement years, Lindgren had four bouts of pneumonia in five years; she realized that she had to take some action. She realized that the lung problems she started having at age 62 could be linked to the sedentary lifestyle she led since her retirement. She understood that she had to change her habits of just sitting around doing the usual senior pastimes of reading, knitting and writing.

• **STRENGTH TO PROVIDE** •

Not long after this jabbing stimulus, Mavis' re-awakening was further enhanced when she attended a lecture given by a health expert in her locality. She realized she had to take responsibility for her own health. She decided to follow the advice of her doctor and enrolled in an Early Bird Walking program. When she first started the program, Mavis had to take the walking slowly because of her weak heart, arthritic frame, and somewhat atrophied muscles. She also had to consider that she was twenty pounds overweight due to her previous inactive lifestyle. But with persistence, the incapacitating factors became re-enforced support, and Mavis walked off those twenty pounds! It was a turning point in Mavis' life.

Within a few years, Mavis experienced the re-birth of her health. Gradually, with improved endurance, Mavis moved from walking to jogging and then to running. This really worked even more wonders for her health. She recalled that, after she started running, she never had another cold which was a significant upgrading of her health status. Mavis had brought forth her dream of good health and fitness.

THE STRENGTH TO PROVIDE FOR A NEWLY RE-BORN HEALTH

Having acquired the strength to bring forth her desired standard of health, Mavis recognized that she needed to nurture it. She needed to take ownership of this newly delivered dream of sound health. She knew it would be wise to take care of it to ensure that it did not decrease or even get annihilated. It would have been very sad to return to poor health after this victory she had. Therefore, Mavis continued with the running, gradually increasing her time and building more endurance. By the time she was 70, Mavis had taken on marathon races. She trained an average of 50 miles a week. She broke world records in the 26-mile Portland Marathon for different age categories. She continued to find strength to provide for her good health.

This was empowering for Mavis as she attracted attention to her achievements. The race organizers bought into her determination and strength of spirit. Each year at the marathon races, they allowed her to wear the jersey number that indicated her age at the time. Thus, as Lindgren nurtured her dream of health, she also increased her strength to celebrate. This further enhanced her taking ownership of her dream.

Mavis' strength to nurture her good health has resulted in an amazing level of fitness as depicted by the functioning of her body organs. When physiological tests were performed to check the benefits of her lifestyle of running, it was found that when Mavis was 80, her heart and lung efficiency were that of a normal 22 year old woman! The test results also showed that her body composition then was at 12% fat whereas a normal healthy college-age woman has 25% fat body composition while the average middle age woman has 32% fat. Running had turned Mavis into a fit, lean octogenarian.

INSPIRING OTHERS TO TAKE RESPONSIBILITY FOR THEIR HEALTH

Mavis' lifestyle of maintaining her good health has been celebrated in many circles. She has appeared on a number of TV and radio shows serving as inspiration to others. She has been featured in magazines such as The New York Times, Runner's World and Sports Illustrated which captioned her as 'Amazing Mavis' (4). Lindgren's strength to provide for her dream feeds her strength to celebrate, thereby empowering her. As people admire her strength, they are inspired to take responsibility for their own health as well.

Mavis never gave up on nurturing her good health. She kept running in marathon races until age 90 when she retired after the 1997 Race (5-6). During this last race, the strength to celebrate that she had acquired over the years shone through. Her two daughters and grandchildren accompanied and gave her their support. Many adoring fans in her community of Portland, Oregon turned out to cheer their star. Many of these fans can testify to the fact that Mavis did not only nurture her good health, but also inspired them to do the same. Lindgren's influence reached international circles as she inspired people from different nations to change their own health through taking responsibility for it. She inspired them to discover the strength to bring forth a dream of good health and fitness and maintain it thereafter.

Nurturing and providing for your newly delivered dream is a way to ensure its continued existence. To make certain that the new status that you acquired as a result of your dream achievement does not revert back to its old status; you need to keep cultivating it. When your new dream becomes well established and is on a solid footing, you are able to take on more new dream concepts. With your reinforced new status, you are able to launch forth new action steps and goals for new dreams. You are able to multiply your dream's fulfillment.

CHAPTER 12

Strength to Multiply
Reproducing your dream fulfillment

I n the earlier chapters of this book, I focused on how to breathe new life into a vital dream, which you previously abandoned. I also discussed how to re-conceive that dream in the light of your new circumstances and then launch new goals and action steps towards fulfilling it. In addition, I discussed how to grow your dream concept, protrude it and ultimately give birth to it. The two previous chapters dealt with the aspect of taking ownership of your newly delivered dream through celebrating and providing for it.

When you have given your dream appropriate nurturing, your new status is reinforced. Then you will be in a position of starting the cycle all over again. You will be ready to reproduce the various phases of dream fulfillment. You will be in top gear to multiply your dream accomplishments.

WHAT IS IT TO MULTIPLY YOUR DREAM ACHIEVEMENT?

Multiplying your dream achievement simply means increasing the number of dreams you realize. This concept is applicable to any category of dreams. For a couple who just realized their family dream through the birth of their first child, the strength to multiply comes into force when they decide to have their second child. They may choose to go through the whole process of conception to child birth many times over. It all depends on their desire as regards family size. Their family dream is multiplied as they have two or more children.

Multiplication is a way of life. Living objects grow through multiplication of cells. And this multiplication is a result of nourishment. Multiplication is thus an outcome of proper nurture and care. Multiplication is achieved through reproducing what is already in existence to get more of that same thing. Reproducing a dream achievement means making a replica of it by repeating the process in view of obtaining a similar result. The career person can multiply their career fulfillment as they move from one job to another while they remain in that career field. Their career dream is multiplied as they have new opportunities to demonstrate their expertise with different organizations over successive periods of growth. The new professor who published his first research paper while he was still a graduate student achieved a highly desirable dream in academic circles. However, he does not stay put on the dream achievement of that singular paper. Usually, he looks for multiplication of his dream and sets new goals towards publishing a second paper. And if he holds on to his bigger goals, he would have multiple numbers of peer-reviewed academic papers in his name over the course of his academic career. Thus his dream fulfillment is multiplied.

MULTIPLYING IS LIKE SETTING UP A CHAIN REACTION

Multiplying a dream fulfillment can also be compared to a chain reaction that leads to a cascading effect. In basic chemistry, a chain reaction is one in which a product of the reaction is itself a reactive particle which can cause more similar reactions. Often, when the first few dreams that are vital to your life's mission are fulfilled, the stage is set for more dreams to be fulfilled. In many cases, once the first vital dream is fulfilled it serves as a stimulus that sets up a chain reaction. This reaction can set off more dreams being fulfilled resulting in a cascade of dreams being achieved. A cascade indicates a surge, gushing out or spilling over of an object or event. And the multiplication of dreams can reach an extent where you have a surge or spilling over of accomplishments. Such a mighty outpour of dream achievements ultimately leads to a fulfilled life.

This analogy of multiplying of dream achievements is vivid in the case of business dreams. Many entrepreneurs struggle through the growth process of a dream while realizing their first ten thousand in profit margin. When they achieve this dream of their first ten thousand and nurture it, this realized dream is often the stimulus for more new dream achievements being realized. That first bulk profit margin and the publicity attached to the process of achieving it often creates a business environment and opportunities whereby multiples of that amount is realized.

All of these examples demonstrate that seeking to multiply your dream fulfillment is a desirable goal. It is rational to find means of acquiring the strength to multiply.

ACQUIRING THE STRENGTH TO MULTIPLY

In Chapter 2, I discussed the dream gestation cycle which illustrated the various steps towards bringing forth your dream. The dream cycle is a revolving one, implying that you can revive an interrupted dream and pass it through the cycle again. That means you re-conceive it, grow and protrude it, bring it forth and then nurture it. Figure 2.1 illustrates that you may have new interruptions in your dream pursuit at any point in the cycle. In fact, your dream may be interrupted at delivery point. However, at whichever stage your hold-up occurs, when you decide to revive the dream, it is essential to re-conceive the dream before starting new action towards it. This is because your circumstances might have changed since you last worked on the dream goals. Thus, the conception stage can be regarded as the starting point for any type of dream pursuits.

When it comes to multiplying your dream fulfillment, the conception point is also the starting point. And then you will need to move that new concept through the dream gestation cycle all over again. Having the strength to multiply implies having the capacity to go through the process of dream pursuit many times over. However, the good thing is that you can tap into your experience when you begin your journey for multiplying your dream. But, the fact still remains that you have to start at the very beginning. You have to get pregnant again with new dream concepts.

GETTING PREGNANT WITH NEW DREAM CONCEPTS

As I discussed in Chapter 6, getting pregnant with dream concepts requires you to be in a right frame of mind. When it comes to reproducing your recent dream accomplishment, the likelihood of getting pregnant again begins with an awareness of your new position. You have recently reached the realm of dream achievers. You have had a first-hand experience of your capability. You have been empowered. You recognize that the sky is the limit. This frame of mind should get you excited about visions of even a greater future. It is the right frame of mind that is conducive for new dream conceptions.

The other means for conceiving new ideas is to have items and events related to that goal in the area of your central vision. Your new dream achievement is a good event in this regard. The recently delivered dream can be the stimulus for those new concepts. As you nurture your new dream, you will be open to seeing new concepts arising from it. Taking care of that dream will cast visions of even bigger goals in similar areas.

Thus, this new conception should be more forthcoming than the first one. You have already overcome obstacles to conception such as fear and negative mindset the first time around. You may have proven that you cannot be confined by walls of tradition or culture. You have recognized that going big and wild in your imaginations is a positive way of dreaming. All in all, you are in a much better position to conceive towards multiplying your dream fulfillment.

GROWING, PROTRUDING AND GIVING BIRTH THE SECOND TIME AROUND

Having conceived your new dreams, and being equipped with the first dream you have recently achieved, you are ready to launch new action goals towards your new dream journey. You can tap into your previous action steps and SMART goal setting. As discussed in Chapter 7, during your periodic evaluations of the process, you have learnt what works and what does not. So, you can use the lessons learnt for your new action plan. And it is essential to remember that you are now working in modified circumstances as compared to the first time around. Your new circumstances consist of all that has changed due to your recent dream achievement. Using your new circumstances to your advantage will help you propel the growth and protrusion of this new vision even faster than the first one. Therefore, it is important to launch some new action plans using that newly delivered dream as a solid foundation.

Consider the case of James and Shirley, a retired couple who accomplished their long term leisure dream of traveling to Hawaii not too long ago. After a period of one year of home-based activities, they decided to launch a new leisure dream. This second dream was a trip to Africa. James and Shirley realized that planning for this second trip was more straightforward than the first time around. They had already established a good relationship with the travel agent who helped them in getting the best deals. They were also aware of necessary actions like travel vaccinations, house sitting arrangements and so on. However, they recognized that although their new dream was in the same area of travel and leisure, there were new issues to consider during their planning. There were new destination-related factors to think about while making their travel plans to Africa; a variety of which they did not have to deal with during their Hawaiian trip. In addition, Shirley had undergone a hip replacement surgery during the year after their Hawaii trip. This was a major factor they had to consider during their SMART goal setting.

One other fact to recognize during the pursuit of a second dream is that you may still experience periods of interruptions during the gestation cycle. The fact that you have achieved a dream in a similar area does not mean that you are immune to new interruptions in the journey of a subsequent dream. During the pursuit of your first dream, you were able to use such periods of interruptions as phases of growth. You tapped into the hold-up intervals, using them to work on related goals in complimentary areas that further propagated your dream when you re-launched it. At times, such interruption periods opened doors for new opportunities that eventually lead to growth and protrusion of your dream.

In a similar fashion, you should be open to the positive aspects of any period of delays you may encounter during the pursuit of your second dream.

When you have effectively worked your way through the dream gestation cycle the second time around, you will be ready to bring forth this new dream at the right due date. And then you can go through the process of taking ownership of this second dream by celebrating and nurturing it. This second dream achievement combined with the previous one will now serve as stimuli for even more dream conceptions. Thus the cycle goes round many times, resulting in a multiplication of your dream achievements.

MULTIPLE DREAM ACHIEVEMENTS

Over the centuries, many people have been classified as multiple dream achievers. Their dream accomplishments transpired into many areas such as career, leisure and personal development. Most often such people met with interruptions in the pursuit of their new dreams. However, with the dogged determination, strength and sense of purpose they had acquired from achieving previous dreams, they continued finding new stimulus to revive and give birth to their new dreams.

Many men who have left legacies at the end of their lives all started with fulfilling one essential dream. They overcame all obstacles on their way and did not let go of that essential dream. When that dream was fulfilled, it created for them a chain reaction that led to many more essential dreams being fulfilled. They achieved a multiplying effect. They had the strength to multiply. They had the strength to deliver their life's purpose.

James Hudson Taylor is such a man. He was a man of purpose. His legacy remains with us today.

A DISTINCTIVE SPIRITUAL DREAM

James Hudson Taylor was born in Barnsley, Yorkshire, England in 1832 to parents that identify with the Christian faith. However, early in life, he walked away from that belief (1). At age 17, he received a stimulus that made him re-examine his life's purpose. At the issue of this self-reflecting period, James began to profess and preach faith in Christ. Soon after that, he decided to go to China as a missionary. That was the essence of his life-changing dream.

James had clarity in his dream conception. He knew exactly which career he wanted to pursue and he knew in which country he wanted to perform these duties. Moreover, he knew the specificities of the vision that his dream embraced. He knew that his dream had both a spiritual and career component. James' vision of an ideal future turned out to be one that was intertwined with his life's purpose. It became the pivot on which all other dreams in his life rotated. Taylor's dream guided his relationship, financial, personal development, leisure, and health pursuits. In fact, it became the purpose of his entire life. Hudson Taylor ended up spending 51 of his 73 years' life in China fulfilling that purpose. During that time, he founded the China Inland Mission (CIM) which is still in existence today as OMF (Overseas Missionary Fellowship) International. But how did he get started? What are the interruptions that Taylor faced on the way? How did he grow his dream and bring it forth? What did he do to provide for his dream when it was newly delivered? And how did he achieve such a great multiplying effect of his dream achievement?

EXCEPTIONAL STRATEGIZING AND GOAL SETTING

Soon after his dream conception, Hudson launched out SMART goals and pursued relevant action steps. His interest in missions moved him to study materials about China, his target mission zone. Then he went on to study Mandarin, Greek, Hebrew and Latin. During this initial phase, he associated with people who could influence him positively towards his big dream. These included a medical doctor and Bible teachers of the time. Thus, Taylor used role models and mentors to further his goals.

The first year after his conversion, at age 18, Hudson started studying medicine at the Royal London Hospital, London in preparation for working in China. That was one of his major goals towards his bigger vision. During the course of his studies, the eyes of the world turned to China through the civil war. This led to the creation of the Chinese Evangelization Society. Hudson saw this as an opportunity he could embrace to further his goals towards a mission in China. At the age of 21, he signed up as the first missionary to the Society. This was before the end of his medical studies.

CHINA, HERE I COME!

This must have been a great achievement for Hudson. His dream had finally come true. He headed to China enthusiastic about his vision and carrying medical supplies.

Arriving in China, Taylor was faced immediately with a raging civil war making his first year there chaotic—to say the least. As time passed and the political up-rise settled down, he was able to launch out many preaching tours to Shanghai, his first missionary station. However, he was often poorly received. In fact, Hudson faced an interruption after realizing the major goal of arriving in China. He was there, in China, but the object of his dream—evangelization—was stalled. Hudson designed a strategy to overcome this obstacle. He donned native Chinese clothes and shaved his forehead. This approach made him more accessible to the people. Hudson faced a number of other hindrances in this first missionary visit to China. He was robbed and his medical supplies were destroyed by a fire. This lack of financial resources could have sapped him of the enthusiasm towards his goals. However, Hudson held on to his dream.

He relocated to another region in China called Ningpo. While there, he obtained support from George Muller, another major missionary of his time. Through this support, Hudson was able to resign from the services of the mission society that sponsored him on the trip. At that time it had become problematic for him to keep on working with them. He then launched an independent body called Ningpo Mission.

After this, Hudson fulfilled a number of other dreams that were in line with his big vision. He got married to his first wife, Maria Jane who was also a missionary and they started raising a family. Another

• STRENGTH TO MULTIPLY •

dream that Hudson realized was the taking over of the running of a medical facility in Ningbo. Hence, there was a multiplication of dream fulfillment in Hudson's life.

Not too long afterwards, however, Hudson faced a period of interruption in achieving his big vision. He had to return to England with his family due to poor health.

GROWING THROUGH A PERIOD OF INTERRUPTION

During the six-year period of this delay, Hudson pursued other goals that were directly (or indirectly) related to his bigger vision of being a missionary in China. Hudson completed his medical studies and worked on the translation of the Bible into Ningpo. He also traveled around the British Isles, promoting the needs of China while speaking in churches. During this period of furlough in England (1865), Hudson founded the China Inland Mission (CIM) with other discerning associates. This big step was a great spur, a catalyst towards achieving his big vision—the evangelization of China. With the new CIM, Hudson was able to get more workers (24, at first) to the mission field. He was also able to raise financial resources to achieve his vision. When Hudson and his family returned to China for their second visit six years later, he was better equipped to carry out his life's mission. He had acquired more strength to deliver.

Hudson multiplied his dreams fulfillment along the journey. He met with more obstacles and faced losses such as the death of his first wife. He re-married and continued moving forward with his life's mission. At the end of his life, Hudson had carried out eleven major missionary stays in China. In 1905, Hudson died and was buried in China, the place where his whole life's mission was orchestrated and carried out.

Ruth Tucker, an historian, claims that *'no other missionary in the nineteenth centuries since the Apostle Paul has had a wider vision and carried out a more systematic evangelism plan of evangelizing a broad geographical area than Hudson Taylor'* (2).

MULTIPLE DREAM ACHIEVEMENT LEADING TO A LEGACY

Hudson passed on his missionary legacy to his family. Many generations of James Hudson Taylor continue his full-time ministry today in Chinese communities in Hong Kong and Taiwan. The Rev. James Hudson Taylor III and his son, the Rev. James Hudson Taylor IV, are now based in Hong Kong, providing full-time Chinese ministries.

The life of James Hudson Taylor has also inspired people in many generations to follow his example of service and sacrifice. Such include Olympic Gold Medalist Eric Liddell, and international evangelist Billy Graham.

In addition, the legacy of the missionary organization founded by Hudson (CIM) remains today as OMF International. The CIM is known to have brought over 800 missionaries to China, which started 125 schools (3). Their work resulted in 18,000 Christian conversions, and the establishment of more than 300 work stations with more than 500 helpers in 18 provinces (4).

Yes, James Hudson Taylor is one man who had the strength to multiply his dream's fulfillment and hence the strength to deliver his life's mission. And the legacy he left continues to multiply that dream today. His story demonstrates the fact that the multiplication factor, which you can realize when you pursue your dream wholeheartedly, is limitless.

THE STIMULUS OF A LIFE TRANSITION

Multiplication of dreams is not only associated with career dreams. It is a phenomenon that applies to dreams that are essential to the life's purpose of any individual. When someone is at a crossroad point in his/her life, it becomes critical for that person to fulfill one essential dream. It may seem that the fulfillment of that dream will determine whether that individual is going to make it or not. After a life-changing event, the ability to effectively launch forward and realize a vital goal is often the turning point to an upward movement. The achievement of that vital dream could result in a dramatic transformation of the status of the individual. And, as mentioned above, the realization of that dream could serve as a stimulus for reproducing their dream's fulfillment and ultimately multiplying it. Therefore, acquiring the strength to multiply could result from a single dream achievement that takes place after a life-altering event.

Consider the case of a divorced woman whose economic status was downgraded after her marriage ended. She struggles to achieve a breakthrough that will reverse her economic status for good. She conceives a vision of an ideal future that, among other things, consists of financial independence. Such is the kind of motivation behind the story of Eula McClaney (5). It is the story of a woman who fulfilled a dream of financial independence after her divorce. This led to a multiplication effect that is evident in her family today.

A POOR FAMILY HERITAGE

Eula McClaney had a poor family heritage at birth. She was one of three children born to sharecropper parents in 1913 in Troy, Alabama (6). The family lived in a wooden shack with no plumbing. They picked cotton for a living and Eula was drafted into this miserable income earning process when she could barely walk. Eula was very diligent in her duties being even harder working than her brothers were. She managed to attend school but only completed the sixth grade. She never had a chance to attend college. When she got married at age 19, her father was disappointed for losing a very good field hand.

Years later, Eula's family moved from Alabama to Pittsburgh where her husband, Burnish, had obtained some work with a steel company. Eula also started helping Burnish in some of his additional part-time jobs of painting. However, this did not work well with Eula's body. She started having back problems. Therefore, she decided to engage in other means of income earning. She started baking home-made goods and sold them. With the help of her daughters who hawked the goodies, this new venture provided some money to boost the family income.

With this kind of background, it was obvious that Eula's family experienced significant financial struggles. The turning point in Eula's life came when she met a real estate broker who informed her of the lucrative possibilities available through real estate investments. Eula's strengths as a hard worker came into play when she decided to tap into this new opportunity.

A REAL ESTATE DREAM

Eula worked hard and saved enough money ($1500) to buy their first family home in Pittsburgh. This investment marked the beginning of the upturn of events for Eula and her family. She decided to reproduce this dream of real estate ownership by gradually purchasing more properties. About nine years after her first real estate purchase,

Eula had purchased 33 units in Pittsburgh. She also diversified into a stock investment that turned out to be highly profitable. Thus, Eula began to multiply her dream fulfillment through solid investment strategies.

However, 25 years into her marriage, Eula and Burnish headed for the divorce courts. This resulted in a down turn of events in Eula's financial independence. She lost a huge amount of money. Nevertheless, she did not allow this major life-changing event to hold her back. Eula pulled herself together again and revived her dream of being financially independent.

Eula had relocated to California with her two daughters before the divorce. At 44, Eula had to re-launch new goals and action steps towards her dream. She purchased a motel and started all over again. She ran the motel and her daughters helped out in working on the premises and at some other outside jobs. Through their hard work, Eula and her daughters were able to save quite a bit of money. Then, they went back into real estate investments. Gradually, they started increasing their number of acquisitions. Thus, despite the interruption caused by her divorce, Eula's revived dream was brought forth the second time around. And she recovered her strength to multiply her dream of financial independence.

A CROSS ROAD DREAM FULFILLMENT GOT MULTIPLIED MANY TIMES OVER

The McClaney family eventually realized a fortune in real estate investments in California and in six states across the United States. Their original investment has become a multimillion dollar real estate empire. Today, Eula's daughter, Doris, runs that empire.

Therefore, Eula's dream for financial independence, which was realized the second time around yielded much more multiples than the first time she birthed her dream. Eula, through her hard work, determination and persistence, had the strength to deliver her dream of financial independence and many multiples of it are still evident today.

Both James Hudson Taylor and Eula McClaney had the strength to multiply their dream fulfillment while they were still living. They multiplied their dream fulfillment in the short term. That strength to multiply they had during their life time has been passed down to their offspring and continues to yield more strength to multiply today. Their original short-term strength to multiply has been transformed to long-term strength to multiply in the form of their legacies.

FINDING IT DIFFICULT TO MULTIPLY YOUR DREAM ACHIEVEMENTS?

Despite all of the exciting advantages attached to multiplying your dream's fulfillment, it is possible that you are finding it difficult to acquire the strength to multiply your dream achievement. This could be due to a number of reasons:

- You are stuck on your previous dream achievement. Maybe because you are 'too attached' to it. That looks like the proverbial story of a woman who is too attached to her baby, even when it has grown up. The woman does not want to have another baby for fear of competing attention with her first child.
- You lost your new dream conception soon after you started working hard on your action steps. This may be the result of not having an adequate rest period after the first dream achievement.

- You have lost interest in the dream because no one appreciated your efforts the first time around. Or maybe you are facing other forms of peer pressure that makes you feel there is no point in continuing on that path.

In order to overcome the above objections and other reasons for your inability to multiply your dream's fulfillment, you need to see beyond your first dream achievement. You need to recognize that no matter how great that achievement was, there is even more to life. Bringing forth additional dreams will enrich your life even further.

Here are some tips that should help you achieve a cascade of dream fulfillment as you reproduce your recent dream achievement.

ENSURING THAT YOU HAVE THE STRENGTH TO MULTIPLY YOUR DREAM

1. Celebrate and take ownership of the first dream achievement.

When you stand in time, and deliberately acknowledge your previous achievement, you will be able to move forward with more vigour. When you have savoured the moment of your achievement in different ways, you will not get stuck with that achievement. You will be able to move forward from it because you have created memories of it in various ways, which will be useful for the future. If you take time to celebrate, even if you did not receive support from some people, you are putting yourself in charge of the future. Your dream multiplication process is part of that future. Do not let other people's opposing opinion hinder you from taking charge of it.

2. Take time to nourish your newly delivered dream.

When you nurture your first dream, you will get to cherish it even more. When you nourish your dream, you are creating an environment conducive to duplicating it. The nourished dream can serve to spur the opening of new doors of opportunities that will work towards its multiplication. Therefore, nurturing your first dream is a vital part of acquiring the strength to multiply it.

3. Leave a breathing space between your first dream achievement and your new dream conception.

Fatigue is a killer of good intentions. When you rest appropriately after the major process of bringing forth your first dream, you will have enough time to build-up a reserve of resources towards the next dream process. You will need reserves of physical, intellectual and other forms of strength for your second dream. Having enough of the strengths will help towards ensuring that your second dream does not die before you birth it. It will help ensure that the dream delivery is replicated.

4. Continue to align your values with your life's purpose.

As discussed in Chapter 4, when you have your dreams in sync with your purpose in life, the probability of reproducing that dream is higher. If your pursuits are not in alignment with your purpose, dreams that are achieved may be isolated. It becomes difficult to connect your life-lines with one another, and this is essential to the multiplication of your dream.

The story of James Hudson Taylor (above) illustrates this principle vividly. If James did not align his academic goals towards his life's purpose, it might have been difficult for him to multiply his dream's fulfillment. Becoming a doctor opened doors to many opportunities for him in his missionary endeavours. In addition, it would have been highly improbable for him to achieve so great a multiplication factor if he married someone who did not buy into his idea of being a missionary

5. Team up with discerning associates.

All through the various stages of the dream delivery journey, it is useful to join efforts with other individuals who will help you further your goals. This is also very important when it comes to multiplying your dream's fulfillment. There is a boosting of your efforts and resources when you collaborate with appropriate partners and this will enhance your dream multiplication process.

Multiplying a dream's fulfillment in one area of life is a great thing. Because you have achieved many dreams in one area, it is easy for you to cast even bigger goals in that same area. You have mastered that field of knowledge and you are fully aware of what it takes to move your ideas along from conception to delivery. However, life is not just composed of one field of knowledge or site of growth. And just as there are many areas in life, so are there many categories of dreams, which you can realize. Therefore, in addition to having the strength to multiply your dream's fulfillment in one category, it is desirable to have dreams' fulfillments in all areas of your life. It is good to have the strength to deliver on an all-round basis.

CHAPTER 13

Strength to Deliver
Becoming an all-round dream achiever

In the preceding chapters of this book, I have discussed the process of picking up a dream or a goal that you previously abandoned, revitalizing it, re-conceiving it, growing it and ultimately giving birth to it. I also discussed the concepts of celebrating your new accomplishment, taking ownership of it by providing for it and going further in realizing more dreams and goals. The whole process of dream realization is a journey just like that of childbirth, the imagery of which I have used to illustrate the concepts.

This chapter is a summary of the steps previously explained.

The word 'deliver' in this chapter represents the whole journey from conception to bringing forth your previously interrupted dream. It also includes the process of nurturing and providing for it as well as reproducing it to get multiple dream achievements. In essence the word 'deliver' is used here in terms of producing results, attaining a desired state, achieving a desired goal, accomplishing a desired feat, pulling off a great event or performance, or realizing a desired dream.

THE ABILITY TO DELIVER YOUR LIFE MISSION

In Chapter 3, I mentioned that the term 'strength to deliver' is used in many industries to describe the capacity to perform and the ability to produce desired results. The term is used for individuals ranging from school teachers to political leaders and company executives. It is also used by bodies as diverse as non-profit organizations, engineering companies and financial institutions. In addition, I discussed how, as an individual, you too need the 'strength to deliver' your mission in life. You need the ability to achieve goals in line with your life's purpose. You need the capacity to multiply your dream's fulfillment in all areas of your life. The strength to deliver your life's mission in the long run leads to a fulfilled life. Having the strength to deliver makes your life more meaningful. When you have the strength to deliver, you can look forward to the next day with enthusiasm. You have an increased zest for life. That's the crux of the discussion in this book. And that strength to deliver in the long run starts with fulfilling one dream at a time.

FULFILLING ONE DREAM AT A TIME

Your interrupted dream could be in the category of personal development. You always wanted to play the guitar and started off with a semester's lessons, but you quit midway. Your vision of an ideal future could be in the area of career or finances. Maybe you started working towards becoming financially independent. You could have had a goal of having substantial investment savings towards retirement. On the other hand, your dream could be a health or fitness one. You always wanted to be fit and have endless energy to carry out your routine duties. You may also have had a public service dream. You wanted to start a foundation to help inner city kids who are struggling with their education. You could have had a leisure dream such as traveling to Peru to see Machu Picchu.

It does not matter what category your dream belongs to. If it is a dream that is intertwined with your life's purpose, once you have been able to revive it in the light of your new circumstances and give birth to it, you have achieved one major goal in your life. In addition, the process of taking ownership of that dream after birthing it will help you cherish it and look forward to having more of it. When you nurture your dream, when it is newly delivered, you will be in the proper position to reproduce it over and over again.

If that dream is truly an important aspect of your life's mission, when you have achieved multiples of it, it tends to spill into other areas of your life. In essence, that means you will be able to take on new dream concepts in other categories, work on them and ultimately give birth to them. For instance, if your first dream achievement multiples are in the area of career, you could take on new dream concepts in your relationship or family life. While aligning your goals with your life's mission, these dreams being fulfilled in the second and subsequent categories could be reproduced and multiplied as well. In that case, you would have been able to diversify your portfolio of dream achievements.

DIVERSIFIED PORTFOLIOS AND FINDING BALANCE IN LIFE

Financial advisors always suggest to the new long-term investor to have a mix of investment funds in their portfolio. This is so because there are different levels of risks attached to each type of funds in a portfolio. On the other hand, some funds trade better than others. There are in fact many factors that influence the returns received on long-term investments. Having diversified funds in one's portfolio ensures that there is a balance in the overall risk for the long-term investment. The purpose of the diversification is to ensure that, whichever way the market goes, the investment will yield a positive return. Thus, diversification is about achieving a balance towards a positive return.

Achieving balance is also very important in life. If you have all of your dream achievements in only one area of life, you are a dream achiever. You may enjoy your dream's fulfillment for a given period. However, if you just focus on this one area of life and neglect other areas for a long period, your life may become skewed or unbalanced. If all of your dream achievements are only in an area of personal development, and for many years, you do not work on any relationship or family goals, your fulfillment will not carry through. To continue to have the zest for life, you need to find a balance in your dream achievements through diversification into all areas of life. When you have been able to diversify your dream's fulfillment into other areas of your life you will become an all-round dream achiever.

STRENGTH TO DELIVER ON AN ALL-ROUND BASIS

Becoming an all-round dream achiever, therefore, begins with having the strength to deliver that one essential or set of dreams intertwined with your life's purpose. And, as I discussed in Chapter 4, for you to know which dream is interlocked with your mission, you need to first discern your life's purpose.

When you have discovered your life's purpose and have effectively delivered a dream that is intertwined with that purpose, over time, the overall result gets multiplied many times over. In fact, the results spill out into various aspects of your life. When you have become an all-round dream achiever, you need to keep aligning your new goals towards your life's purpose. This will help ensure that the dream achievements will carry on through your life time. And if you have carried other people in your circle of influence along with you during those accomplishments, your dream achievements could be passed on as a legacy to future generations.

Having the strength to deliver on an all-round basis is a great goal to work towards. And as mentioned above, it all starts with delivering one dream at a time. In order to sum up what it takes to deliver one dream, let's look at a brief summary of the dream gestation cycle.

In Chapter 2, I classified the stages of the dream gestation cycle into three parts. These are the steps involved in:
- reviving an interrupted dream and clarifying your vision,
- rebuilding and growing your dream by taking new action steps and goals towards its delivery, and
- reproducing the dream birthing process to get multiples of dream accomplishments.

For ease of discussion, I have summarized the concepts required for delivery of your dream under these three categories. However, most of the insights are relevant to more than one aspect of the overall process. In fact, many strategies offered in the various sections apply to all three parts of the process.

WHAT DOES IT TAKE TO REVIVE A DREAM?

Reviving an interrupted dream involves incorporating issues from these three parts of your life to produce a desired course of action:

- Your past
- Your present
- Your future

Breathing new life into a deserted dream revolves around carrying out a mental examination of your past in order to draw useful lessons from it for the present and the future. This recollection of past events takes into account both your successes and your failures as there are always useful insights to draw from these divergent situations.

Before you can revitalize your old dream, you also need to consider your present situation in terms of your strengths and your mission in life. You need to have an accurate picture of how your strengths can be used towards living out your purpose. And the process of reviving will be incomplete unless you use the knowledge of your past and present to cast a vision of the ideal future that you desire. This involves using your imagination to transport yourself from where you are currently to where you want to be in the future.

The following is a summing up of insights to help you towards successful reviving of your abandoned dreams.

1. Recognize and acknowledge your uniqueness.

When you embrace your distinctiveness, it will help you focus on the essentials, ignore the irrelevant and have enough strength to cast the vision of the future you desire. When you know who you are, you will be able to clarify what you really want in life.

2. Take your position in the driver's seat.

Since this dream is your concept, you will have to be in the lead as regards everything that is related to it. You will have to steer the ship on the course you desire. No one else is going to do it for you. And no one can do it in the way you can. Take charge and take control of your vehicle.

3. Forgive the past.

Forgive people who hurt you in the past. Forgive the circumstances that led to that apparent failure during your first attempt at delivering your abandoned dream. Re-analyze the circumstances carefully and view them as part of the womb for your present and future success. Do not burn bridges behind you. People who were not so helpful in the past may turn out to be useful in the future.

4. Channel your anger about the past into a positive path.

If you are holding a significant amount of displeasure about some events in your past, instead of getting hurt by it, use it as a stimulus to cast a vision for a better future. Direct that anger into a means of setting higher goals that you can achieve in your present circumstances.

5. De-clutter your life and environment.

If you are to see clearly into what you desire for the future, you need to remove items that are blocking your view. You also need to stop associations that are making your life miserable. Consider your options carefully and always go for an environment where your dream concept has higher chances of survival.

6. Focus on your strengths and not your weaknesses.

Know your limitations, but do not capitalize on them. Build your confidence by looking at your successes in the past. Have faith in yourself that you are able to accomplish unimaginable feats.

7. Surround yourself with discerning companions.

Mentors, coaches and people who have been on the path before and have your best interest at heart are helpful resources. Listen to their advices, process and customize them to your own particular situation. Coaches could guide you and serve as your accountability partners through the process.

WHAT ARE THE NECESSARY REBUILDING FACTORS TOWARDS BIRTHING A DREAM?

The rebuilding part of the dream journey starts with the first set of actions and goals towards moving the dream from an idea to reality. This part of the overall process consists of:

- acquiring knowledge,
- planning and strategizing,
- gathering resources,

- a substantial amount of actions and
- a considerable amount of evaluation or feedback.

Here are some useful guidelines to help you through this part of the cycle:

1. Ensure that you have the right directions.

Make sure that you have the correct information towards your dream pursuit in your present circumstances. Recognize that the information you gathered before your dream was interrupted may be out of date and irrelevant. Always use only the authentic intellectual and physical sources for acquiring the knowledge towards your dream. This will help towards ensuring that the directions you are using are up to date and accurate.

2. Take ownership of your resources.

Firstly, enlist all of the resources that you already have. If such resources had been lying fallow or lent to somebody else during the period of interruption of your dream, you need to regain control over them.

Secondly, if you do not have the resources required, find means of obtaining them in timely manner to fit your plan for your action steps.

3. Take over the writing of your life plan.

Since you understand the vision you have cast better than anyone else, you should write the action steps and goals yourself. Do not allow someone else to write your plan for you. Do not use someone else's plan. Take ownership of the process from the outset by drafting your own plan.

4. Perform specific and measurable action steps towards your bigger goals.

In your life's planning process, break down the bigger goals into specific and measurable action steps. Always allocate a target date for the completion of those steps. That way, you are making yourself accountable for carrying them out.

5. Prioritize your goals and action steps and take breathers in between.

In order to have adequate physical energy and other resources for your action steps at the appropriate time, you need to prioritize your actions towards your final goal. Do not overwhelm yourself by taking much more than you can handle. Always take adequate rests between attaining major goals.

6. Be wise in allocating your resources.

You may need to divert your resources to urgent needs during the growth of your dream. You may need more resources at delivery time. Know how to move your resources around towards urgent goals and when and how to re-direct them to other goals.

7. Give your heart to the whole process.

Do not take half-hearted action steps or work towards unclear goals. Realize that taking short cuts may end up in disasters. Do not skip any steps. You can make the process go faster by taking all of the actions and steps in a shorter amount of time. Nevertheless, you can't fast forward the process by jumping over some steps. You need to achieve all of the necessary goals and take all of the actions as you grow your dream. When it comes to the due date of your dream, summon all your strength from your whole being into that action.

8. Do not allow people or events to get in your way.

Exercise wisdom in dealing with opponents or people who would rather see your dream die. Evaluate criticisms and if there are any positive lessons to be learned from them, carry them forward. However, commit to taking your stand for your dream and circumventing opposition on the journey. Get rid of energy drainers. You need your energy directed in a positive manner towards delivering that dream.

9. Know when to change tactics if necessary.

Perform periodic evaluations of the dream journey at appropriate intervals. Use such analysis to discern whether you need to change your course of action at any time. Assess when and where to make changes, ensuring that your dream survives through the growth period and is ultimately delivered.

10. Use any new periods of interruption to your advantage.

Have an open mind to any new hold-ups that you may experience on your dream journey. Be flexible, analyze what is happening through the interruption and carry the lessons learned forward. If necessary, use the period to perform goals in a complimentary area that may subsequently augment your dream process when you re-launch it.

11. Sow into other peoples' lives in a discerning manner.

Offer relevant and meaningful help to others in processes related to bringing forth their dreams. Assist people with your own expertise when they are working towards their goals. When you sow into other peoples' dream journey in a wise way, you will reap the benefits many times over when you are also working on your dream.

12. Collaborate with discerning associates if necessary.

Working with joint venture partners at appropriate phases of the growth of your dream may facilitate its delivery in the long run. Always ensure that you collaborate with people who will enhance your goals and for whom you are also able to provide some help. That way, the association is a healthy one as both parties may reap some benefits from it.

THE IMPORTANCE OF A POSITIVE ATTITUDE

In the earlier chapters of this book, I described the stories of people who had a positive attitude in the course of pursuing their dreams. Such an attitude helped them in forgiving the past, thereby enabling them to see clearly what they wanted to do with their lives. That positive attitude also helped them overcome the challenges presented by the various interruptions they experienced during their dream journeys.

On the other hand, an individual who has a negative attitude about events in his/her past may not be able to have clarity of mind to see the present or envision the future. With such an attitude, the individual may end up not having the strength to deliver in the long run. This is what happened in the case of Michal, a princess in Biblical times.

MICHAL IN THE MIDDLE

Princess Michal was the first wife of King David, a great heroic leader of the Israelites (1). However, that was not how she became a princess. Michal had a royal heritage, being the daughter of King Saul who had preceded David to the throne of Israel. In fact, Michal was a double princess and had the background required for greatness. Nevertheless, events in Michal's life were not always easy to overcome.

Michal was in the middle of two significant rivalries between two different sets of people. In the first place, when Saul was still on the throne, Michal found herself in the middle of a fierce competition between her father, Saul, and her husband, David. Saul had become jealous of David's heroic conquests as a young man. David was favoured by the people of the land because he defeated many more opponents than Saul did. Michal was in a tight spot. In a bid to satisfy his quest for power, Saul grabbed Michal off David, her first husband, and married her to another man. At a later date, this led to a situation where Michal found herself in the middle again.

When Saul died and David became king, David took Michal from her second husband, re-claimed her as his wife and brought her back to his palace. Michal was again in the middle of a second rivalry, which, in this case, was between her first official husband and her second husband.

THE PRINCESS WITH AN ATTITUDE

As David became better established as king, he carried out some reforms towards returning his people to the worship of the true God. One of the steps he took towards this goal was to bring back the Ark—the symbol of worship—to the capital city. David celebrated this significant occasion in a big way with the whole city. It was during this celebration that Michal's attitude of resentment was brought to the surface. Michal could not find any reason to join in the celebrations. In fact, after the day's events, she poured out her resentment towards David in a verbal outrage. This action resulted in a curse being placed on Michal for dishonouring the king and his good intentions of returning his people to the worship of the true God. The curse translated into a sentence of barrenness for Michal, who subsequently was not able to bring forth any children during her lifetime.

It may seem Michal had the right to hold a grudge against David. She had a history of being in the middle of two major rivalries, in both of which David played a part. However, when David brought her back to the palace, Michal had a choice to make. She could let go of her past and seize the new opportunities at hand. After all, David was her first love. She must have had a great dream for their relationship together at the outset. She could have viewed her re-entry into David's life as a point of revival for those dreams she had at the beginning of their marriage. And even more uplifting is the fact that David had officially become the king and was more powerful than when she had first married him. In addition, the issue of her father's rivalry was no longer in play since he had then passed away. Therefore, Michal could have re-conceived her original dream and modified it to fit the context of her now favourable circumstances.

• STRENGTH TO DELIVER •

NO STRENGTH TO BRING FORTH; NO STRENGTH TO DELIVER

The second option open to Michal was that of holding onto the hurt of her past life. She had suffered tremendously from two major rivalries. She might have felt used or trampled upon by the people she loved. So, she could decide not to forgive her past and stay resentful and bitter to the people she perceived were responsible for the hurt.

Michal chose the second option. She remained resentful and bitter towards David and that cost her much more than she imagined. Michal remained locked in her past, holding the hurt in a sacred place in her heart. Michal did not release the hurt and thus could not have clarity of sight for current events. Neither could she envision the plethora of opportunities that were open to her as the First Lady of one of the greatest kings of that period.

Michal's inability to conceive, a natural childbirth issue, transpired into many aspects of her life. It translated into her inability to deliver in terms of realizing her goals and objectives. It translated into her inability to deliver dreams of various types—family, legacy, spiritual and spousal relationship. Michal's loss of strength to produce biological children translated into her inability to fulfill her life's mission. She was unable to propagate her royal heritage and leave a significant legacy for future generations. Michal lost her strength to deliver because of the negative attitude she had developed and nurtured over time.

It is essential that you maintain a positive attitude as you seek the strength to deliver in all areas of your life. Letting go of the past and seeing new opportunities in the present and the future is a vital tool towards becoming an all-round dream achiever.

WHAT DOES IT TAKE TO REPRODUCE A DREAM MANY TIMES OVER?

The third part of the dream cycle is an enhancement process. It is a great achievement to realize one major goal. However, in order to have a fulfilling life, it is essential to be able to reproduce your dream accomplishment and reap multiples of it over the course of your lifetime.

Obtaining multiples of your dream achievement involves:
- Taking ownership of your first dream achievement
- Using the dream as stimulus for new dream conception, growth and delivery
- Finding balance in life through diversification of your dream accomplishment into all areas of your life.

In addition to the strategies listed above for the first two parts of the dream process, the following is a synopsis of tactics to guide you in reproducing your dream accomplishment.

1. Take time to celebrate and nurture your first dream achievement.

This will help create memories that you can carry forward into the future. Such can serve as stimulus for new dream conceptions. In addition, nurturing your dream will help you cherish it and look forward to more achievements.

2. Recognize the uniqueness of each dream.

Different categories of dreams require different amounts and variety of strengths to bring forth. The type of strength required for a relationship dream differs from that of a leisure dream. Learn to use the appropriate mix of strengths towards the different types of dreams.

3. Align your goals with your life's mission.

When your action steps for each dream are aligned with your mission in life, achieving a dream may result in the simultaneous achievement of a second dream in another area of your life. Lining up your goals with your purpose will ensure that you are connecting lines from one area of your life with another. This will facilitate the spilling over effect of dream achievements.

4. Be focused and flexible.

Be focused but willing to diversify while seeking to achieve a particular dream. In the realization of a financial goal, you may need to work on a career goal first. Be willing to take on complimentary but different goals in other areas towards the ultimate achievement of your dream.

5. Maintain a positive attitude and be persistent.

In some phases of your dream journey, you may achieve a significant number of goals towards achieving your dream. At other times, you may experience a delay or slowing down in the number of achievements. Whatever the situation, always maintain a positive attitude. Never give up on your dream.

6. Enjoy your journey towards dream achievements.

It is always good to look forward with anticipation at the end of the dream journey. However, you need to maintain a positive attitude towards the journey that leads to that end point. The memories you create as you go along are all vital aspects of your dream being achieved. Enjoy the exciting periods when you realize your goals, but maintain an open mind about the challenging periods as well. Recognize that the journey itself makes you grow as a person. Your life will be more fulfilling if you view it that way.

Multiple dream achievements could be realized in any field. The same principles, which apply to reproducing leisure dreams, apply to highly sophisticated dreams such as going into space. Not many people have achieved the latter dream. Among the few people who have realized the dream of traveling to another planet, even a fewer number have been able to reproduce it many times over. One of the significantly few people is Franklin Chang-Díaz.

EARTHLY LANGUAGE CANNOT POSE A BARRIER TO AN OUTER SPACE VISION

Franklin Chang-Díaz (2—3) was born in Costa Rica in 1950. At the age of seven, Franklin's mother told him that the Russians had launched *Sputnik 1*, the first man-made satellite to orbit the Earth. This news spurred Franklin to climb up a mango tree where he watched the sky for hours. This experience was the stimulus for a dream that Franklin conceived since then. He started to wonder about life in space. He always imagined he could go up there and actually experience such a life.

Over the course of his high school education, Franklin's imagination began to run wild and the dream of becoming an astronaut became more fascinating. He realized that the obvious pathway to getting anywhere close to realizing that dream was to go to the United States.

• STRENGTH TO DELIVER •

He explored the idea and started saving towards a trip to the US. Franklin started his journey into the unknown. He arrived in the United States in 1968 with only fifty dollars ($50)! What's more, he could not speak English. Chang-Díaz was quite determined to find a way out. He convinced the administrators of Hartford Public High School to enrol him as a high school senior.

Franklin failed his classes in the first two quarters. However, he would not let this failure be an obstacle in the pathway towards achieving his dream. In the following two quarters, he scored excellent grades, enough to earn him a full scholarship to the University of Connecticut. Franklin acquired more strength to grow action steps towards his dream.

A UNIQUE STRENGTH FOR A UNIQUE DREAM

In 1973, Chang-Díaz graduated with a Bachelor of Science degree in Mechanical Engineering. He went on to the Massachusetts Institute of technology (MIT) where he bagged a Ph.D. in Applied Plasma Physics in 1977. Franklin had an unwavering commitment to learning. He always wanted to learn and understand more. This strength combined with the determination to realize his special dream were powerful stimuli for his academic and career achievements.

After leaving MIT, Dr. Chang-Díaz joined the technical staff of the Charles Stark Draper Laboratory where he continued his research in plasmas and fusion technology. In 1980, Chang-Díaz was selected as an astronaut candidate by NASA. This was a moment of great hope for Franklin—being an astronaut, at last!

In August of 1981 Franklin received his astronaut wings. He had acquired the strength to protrude his action steps towards realizing his dream of going into space. The delivery time of that dream was getting really close.

While undergoing astronaut training he participated in the early Space Station design studies. He also went on to lead the astronaut support crew at the Kennedy Space Center, Florida.

IN SPACE AT LAST!

Franklin was designated for his first space shuttle as an astronaut on the STS-61-C Space Shuttle Columbia. On January 12, 1986 the Columbia was launched from the Kennedy Space Center. That was a great opportunity for Franklin to bring forth his long-harboured dream of going into space.

The shuttle space voyage was successful and Franklin spent a total of 6 days, 2hrs. and 3 min. on the mission. Thus, 30 years after the seed of that dream was planted, Franklin gave birth to it, becoming the first Latin American to accomplish such a feat. In fact, he is the only one of 447 million Latin Americans to have conquered space. He had the strength to deliver.

Eventually the wild dream that Franklin had as a young boy came to reality. Franklin recounts (4) that this first experience was absolutely profound for him. He was able to leave the Earth in a shuttle, unbuckle his seat belts and flow into the cabin, look out the window and see the spectacle of our planet in front of his eyes! It was absolutely fabulous. It was a transforming experience for him and he felt he had 'arrived'.

STRENGTH TO MULTIPLY SPACE MISSIONS

Even though that first experience of achieving his long-term dream was fantastic, Franklin did not get stuck with it. Over the course of his NASA career, he has multiplied that strength to deliver space shuttles seven times. When he retired from NASA in 2005, he had accumulated a total of 66 days 18hrs. 16min. in space missions. He had become a veteran in space shuttle missions. In addition, Chang-Díaz is a record holder for the most spaceflights by an astronaut. He shares this record with another astronaut—Jerry Ross.

With these great accomplishments, Chang-Díaz has acquired the strength to celebrate on the occasion of receiving many awards. These include four honorary doctorate degrees from universities across the United States and Costa Rica. His home country has also acknowledged his unique strength to deliver through other awards and recognition such as the Honour Citizen Award by the National Congress. In addition, the Costa Rican National High Technology Center is named after Franklin.

DIVERSIFICATION OF DREAM ACHIEVEMENTS

Franklin's 'space dream' became his life's mission. It has translated into many other areas of his life. He has the passion of developing new ways to make space shuttles easier through revolutionizing rocket engines. After leaving NASA in 2005, with this vision in mind, Franklin launched his own firm, Ad Astra Rocket Company, a rocket propulsion company (5).

Franklin also multiplies the strength to deliver, instilling it into other aspiring young people. He continues to develop this aspect through his Adjunct Professorship at two universities—Rice University and the

University of Houston, both in Houston, Texas.

Franklin Chang-Díaz did not allow a language barrier or the lack of financial resources to prevent him from realizing the greatest dream he had; that of going into space. He worked his way through many obstacles and over the course of his career, has demonstrated a unique strength to deliver his life's mission.

In this chapter, I summarized how to ensure that you have the strength to deliver; that ability to give birth to your interrupted dreams and thereby the competence to fulfill your life's mission.

As you bring forth your dreams one at a time and continue to hold on to your values and sense of purpose, you will see your dream achievements being multiplied. And, as you multiply your dream's fulfillment in one particular area, it is essential to keep aligning your goals with your life's purpose. As you do this, you will be able to diversify your dream achievements into all areas of your life.

With diversified accomplishments, you will become an all-round dream achiever. This will put you in a position where you enjoy a fulfilled life. As your life becomes more fulfilled, your zest for life will increase and may become infectious. You may not be able to keep it to yourself. You will be geared towards sharing it with others and helping to equip them to find their own strength to deliver

CHAPTER 14

Creating a Ripple Effect

Equipping others to find the strength to deliver

In the previous chapters of this book, I discussed what it takes to find strength to revive and give birth to your interrupted dreams. I gave practical and proven tips to guide you through the various stages of the process. I also elaborated on how you can reap multiples of your dream achievements, thereby enjoy a fulfilled life.

I provided time-tested strategies for reviving, realizing and reproducing various categories of dreams. I shared insights on dreams in the category of education, career, personal development, relationship, business, financial, spiritual, health, sports, leisure, public service and legacy.

I have given numerous examples of people from history and contemporary times whose life stories demonstrate that you can find strength to breathe new life into an abandoned dream and ultimately achieve it. These examples are from men and women of different nationalities and different age groups. The common theme to the stories is the ability of these individuals to realize vital life dreams despite the delays or bottlenecks they encountered on the way. And in so doing, these people found the strength to deliver their life's purpose.

A STRENGTH AND SENSE OF PURPOSE THAT CANNOT BE CONTAINED

My mother has many sayings which are part of my memories of growing up. One of her favourites is: 'Joy and happiness cannot be concealed'. How true! If you are truly happy and have a deep sense of joy, it will always be revealed in your attitude or composure.

The strengths and sense of purpose that you discover when you find the strength to deliver your interrupted dream is limitless. It is a strength that cannot be contained. It is a sense of purpose that cannot be concealed. It is a story that you want to share over and over again. It is a strength that spills over into all areas of your life.

This is the case with Stacy Allison, the woman who took a great risk and found her way right to the top of the tallest mountain in the world—Mount Everest.

HOW FAR CAN A WOMAN CLIMB?

On September 29, 1988, Stacy Allison became the first American woman to reach the summit of the Everest (29,028 ft). Stacy's dream was realized after 29 days on the mountain. That victory is an important achievement in the life of a woman who began serious alpine climbing at age 21. It was not Stacy's first shot at summiting the Everest. Stacy had made a first attempt the previous year (1987). However, during that expedition, Stacy was not able to summit because of a heavy storm. She and her team mates were trapped in a snow cave for 5 days. That was a major interruption in Stacy's dream.

Can you imagine! She was almost there. The team had reached the height of 23,500 feet before being hit by the worst storm in four decades. Stacy and her team had to turn back without reaching the summit. It was like a dream lost at the pre-labour period.

However, Stacy did not give up her dream. On her second attempt with a new expedition group, Northwest American Everest Expedition, she realized her dream. Thus, Stacy Allison became the first American woman to summit Mt Everest! That is a huge achievement.

The beauty of Stacy's story goes beyond the greatness of her achievement. The story provides a very strong metaphor of mountain climbing as related to dream achievement.

HOW HIGH SHOULD THE MOUNTAIN OF YOUR DREAM BE?

Dreaming involves casting a vision of a future that is widely unimaginable. When you set up goals towards your dream, you often aim at feats that are beyond the common thought. The questions that come to mind are: How high should the mountain of your dream be? How far can you go with the wildness of your dream?

These questions are even more important when the dream is one that was previously interrupted. It may be a dream that you deserted because of personal circumstances. On the other hand, it may be a dream, which circumstances beyond your control, forced you to abandon. Such interrupted dreams are often perceived as having a higher risk and frequently incur a greater fear of failure than others.

In Chapter 6, I discussed why you should not lower the ceiling of the original dream when you re-conceive it after a period of interruption.

Stacy Allison did not lower the height of the mountain she wanted to summit. No, after her first inability to achieve that height, she launched out with new determination. She continued working towards that very high-reaching goal. She kept up with the original height of the dream, which was climbing all the 29,028 feet to the summit of the Everest. And the fact that she did summit during her second attempt made her the first American woman to perform such a feat. Her name went down in the annals and she is entered in the Guinness Book of World Records. Other American women may continue to try and succeed to summit the Everest but they cannot claim that position of being the first to summit. And that makes a world of difference.

EQUIPPING OTHERS TO FIND THE STRENGTH TO DELIVER

Stacy's dream was one of personal development and leisure. However, the achievement of that dream has spilled over into other areas of her life. Reaching those heights has given her a unique strength and sense of purpose. She understands what it means to conquer one's mountain and that is very relevant to every day living.

Mount Everest, the tallest mountain in the world, is a powerful metaphor. For every one person that summits Mt Everest, three die trying (1). With this enormous risk involved, great teamwork is essential for the survival of the team.

Using such insights from her mountain climbing experiences, today Stacy consults with organizations and big companies equipping leaders for peak performance. Combined with her business acumen, Stacy taps into her enhanced sense of purpose to empower business leaders to conquer their own mountains using team work. Thus, her

• CREATING A RIPPLE EFFECT •

mountain climbing experience has opened more avenues for success in her life (2).

Stacy found the strength to deliver her life's mission. And today she is multiplying that strength by equipping others to find the strength to deliver their dreams.

CREATE A RIPPLE EFFECT!

It is my hope that this book has empowered you to find the strength to revive and deliver your interrupted dream.

I am positive that your newly accomplished dream will set forth a chain reaction in your life of multiplying your fulfilled dreams. As you find the strength to deliver your interrupted dreams, get ready. Get ready to follow Stacy's example of telling others.

When a stone is tossed into a sea, it creates a tiny wave at the point of entry. This first wave is rapidly transmitted on to the next section of the sea, resulting in many more waves. This multiplication of waves is called the ripple effect. How far the waves travel depends on the force created when the stone first hits the surface of the water. Ripples means multiplying the factor created by a first effect.

Get ready to create a ripple effect. Use the strength of your new accomplishment to tell others that they also can find their strength to deliver their dreams. Tell people in your family and neighbourhood. Pass on the message of hope.

Let them know that they can revive and give birth to their interrupted dreams. It does not matter how long they have deserted that dream. It would not even matter what caused the interruption in the first place. Let them know they can!

If your friends, family and colleagues need professional help, point them in the right direction. Help them locate life coaches and other professionals who can equip them with the right tools. Connect them with life coaches who can serve as accountability partners in their quest to revive and give birth to their interrupted dreams.

__Go on and tell others!__
__Create a ripple effect!!__

Notes

CHAPTER 1

1. This story is found in the Holy Bible: Isaiah, Chapter 37 and 2 Kings, Chapters18-20

CHAPTER 2

1. Webster, F. David, and Adeleye, Tolulope, A., *Stay Sane Through Change* (Martinsburg, WV: Holy Fire Publishing, 2005)
2. http://www.nichd.nih.gov/health/topics/Miscarriage.cfm
    Accessed April14, 12
3. Maslow, *A Theory of Human Motivation* (originally published in *Psychological Review*, 1943, Vol. 50 #4, pp. 370-396).

CHAPTER 3

1. Getline, Meryl, *The World At My Feet: The True And Sometimes Hilarious Adventures Of A Lady Airline Captain*
    (City, Province: Lorrie Press: 2004)
2. Getline, Meryl—private conversation.
3. Martin Luther King Jr., *Strength to Love*
4. Webster, F. David, and Adeleye, Tolulope, A., *Stay Sane Through Change* (Martinsburg, WV: Holy Fire Publishing, 2005) pp.191-196

5. Cooper, David C., Gunby, Colette L., Jackson, Wiley, Jr., Long, Eddie L., Walker, Woodrow II, Chand, Samuel R., *Failure: The Womb of Success (Twenty godly men and women who experienced failure tell their success story*

   (City, Province: Mail Publishing Company, 2000)

CHAPTER 4

1. The Biblical story of Samson is found in The Holy Bible; Book of Judges Chapters 13 to 16.
2. Clifton Strengthsfinder® www.strengthsfinder.com
3. Hudson, Fredric M and McLean, Pamela D. *Life Launch: A Passionate Guide to the rest of your life*
4. Rath, Tom, *StrengthsFinder 2.0: A New and Upgraded Edition of the Online Test from Gallup's Now, Discover Your Strengths* (New York: NY, Gallup, 2007)
5. Winseman, Albert L., Clifton, Donald, O., and Liesveld, Curt, *Living your Strengths: Discover your God-given talents and inspire your community* (New York: NY, Gallup, 2003)
6. <http://www.newadvent.org/cathen/10270b.htm> Ed. 1911.

    Accessed: March 29, 12

    Russell. *The Life of Cardinal Mezzofanti*, London, 1858.
    http://how-to-learn-anylanguage.com/e/mezzofanti/biography/index.html

    Accessed: March 29, 08
7. Dreamworks LLC, 2004 Steven Spielberg: *The Terminal*, Movie Home Entertainment, A Parker/MacDonald Production 2004

• NOTES •

CHAPTER 5

1. http://www.answers.com/topic/resuscitation?cat=health
   Accessed: March 15, 08
2. http://www.stressgroup.com/articles/article/1228898/37894.htm
   Accessed: June 27, 12
   http://www.counselling.cam.ac.uk/anger.html
   Accessed: March 27, 08
3. Dr. Lyle Becourtney
   http://www.angermanagementgroups.com/AngerCanBePositive.html
   Accessed: March 29, 08
4. This Biblical account is found in The Holy Bible; Book of 2 Samuel Chapters 6.
5. http://www.steponline.com/everest/beck_weathers.asp
   Accessed: April 18, 08
   http://www.ordinarypeoplecanwin.com/beckweathers.htm
   Accessed: April 18, 08
6. Weathers, Beck, *Left for Dead: My Journey Home from Everest*. Villard, 2000

CHAPTER 6

1. Weihenmayer, Erik, *Touch the Top of the World: A Blind Man's Journey to Climb Farther Than the Eye can See*, Plume, 2002
2. Weihenmayer, Erik & Stoltz, Paul, *The Adversity Advantage: Turning Everyday Struggles into Everyday Greatness*, Fireside, 2007
3. This aspect of the Biblical story of Moses is recorded in the Book of Exodus, in the Holy Bible.
4. National Center for Health Statistics
   Series 23, No. 25; *Fertility, Family Planning, and Reproductive*

Health of U.S. Women: Data from the 2002 National Survey of Family Growth (PHS) 2006-1977

5. http://www.gettingpregnant.co.uk/factsandfigures.htm
   Accessed: April 16, 08

CHAPTER 7

1. http://www.fastcompany.com/magazine/94/open_women-1-5.html
   Accessed: March 16, 08
2. FastCompany.com "25 Top Women Business Builders" May 2005, Issue 94, Page 67
3. http://shoes.about.com/od/designersmanufacturers/p/taryn_rose.htm
   Accessed: March 16, 08
4. Cantando, Mary; *The Woman's Advantage: 20 women entrepreneurs show you what it takes to grow your business.* Chicago: IL Kaplan Publishing, 2006, p48-51.
5. http://www.pregnancydigest.info/pregnancy-stages-first-trimester/
   Accessed: March 14, 08
6. http://www.nichd.nih.gov/health/topics/Miscarriage.cfm
   Accessed: April 14, 08
7. http://www.pregnancydigest.info/pregnancy-stages-second-trimester/
   Accessed: April 14, 08
8. 2007 Australian of the Year Awards recipients, National Australia Day Council
   http://www.australianoftheyear.gov.au/pages/page305.asp
   Accessed: April 16, 08
   http://www.abc.net.au/tv/enoughrope/transcripts/s2016257.htm
   Accessed: April 16, 08

• NOTES •

http://www.abc.net.au/4corners/content/2003/2003728_positions_vacant/int_major.htm
Accessed: April 16, 08

CHAPTER 8

1. http://www.pregnancydigest.info/pregnancy-stages-last-trimester/
   Accessed: April 20, 08
2. http://womenshealthmatters.ca/centres/pregnancy/pregnancy/third.html
   Accessed: April 20, 08
3. http://en.wikipedia.org/wiki/Deborah_Norville
   Accessed: March 31, 08
4. http://www.dnorville.com/stuff/backontrack.php
   Accessed: March 31, 08
5. Deborah Norville; *Back on Track: How to Straighten Out Your Life When it Throws You a Curve* (Simon & Schuster, 1997)
6. Weiss, R.W. (1993) Loss and Recovery, in M.S. Stroebe, Strobe, W. & Hansson, R.O., (Eds) *Handbook of bereavement theory, research and intervention* (pp.271-284), NY Cambridge University press.
7. www.findingnewloveafter50.com
8. Gloria Lintermans and Stolzman, Marilyn, *The Healing Power of Love: Transcending the loss of a spouse to New Love* Sourcebooks Inc.
9. Gloria Lintermans and Stolzman, Marilyn, *The Healing Power of grief: The Journey through Loss to Love and Laughter* Sourcebooks Inc.
10. Gary Young and Young, Kathy, *Loss and Found: how we survived the loss of a young partner*, Calabash Press Calabass, California, 2002
11. http://lists101.his.com/pipermail/smartmarriages/2004-April/001867.html

12. *Second Chances at Love and Marriage,* The News Review—Oregon, April 18, 2004

Elmasry, Faiza, *Love, Dating and Marriage still goals for older Americans,* Voices of America News 19 February, 2008
http://128.11.143.113/english/archive/2008-02/2008-02-15-voa36.cfm?CFID=38815404&CFTOKEN=49025797
Accessed: April 10, 08

CHAPTER 9

1. http://www.nlm.nih.gov/medlineplus/childbirth.html
   Accessed: April 4, 08
2. *Rudy* movie (Tristar Productions, 1993)
3. www.rudyinternational.com
4. Cantando, Mary, *The Woman's Advantage: 20 women entrepreneurs show you what it takes to grow your business.* Chicago: IL Kaplan Publishing, 2006, p.59-63
5. http://www.rotman.utoronto.ca/news/detail.asp?ID=98
   Accessed: May 1, 08
6. http://www.cawee.net/past_walker.html
   Accessed: May 1, 08
7. www.marniewalker.com

CHAPTER 10

1. http://en.wikipedia.org/wiki/Jenny_Wood-Allen
   Accessed: April 1, 08
2. Gareth A. Davis, *London Marathon: Praise pours in for durable Wood Allen* March 23, 2001

• NOTES •

http://www.telegraph.co.uk/sport/main.jhtml?xml=/sport/2001/03/22/somara23.xml

3. Evening Times June 3, 2005 Scotswoman of the Year 2005; Six of the Best
4. http://en.wikipedia.org/wiki/Jaime_Escalante
   Accessed: March 12, 08
5. *Stand and Deliver* movie, (American Playhouse Theatrical Film 1988 Warner Brothers)
6. *Jaime Escalante's Students: Where Are They Now?*
   http://www.thefutureschannel.com/jaime_escalante/jaime_escalante_students.php
   Accessed: April 2, 08

CHAPTER 11

1. Legson Kayira, *I Will Try* (Doubleday, 1965)
2. Legson Kayira, *Journey to glory and death*
   http://www.time.com/time/magazine/article/0,9171,873347,00.html
   Accessed: April 16, 08
3. Miller, Betty Jean (1988-05-30). *Unhappy with Public Education, She Founded a Christian School. St. Petersburg Times.* Retrieved April 13, 2007 from Lexis Nexis Academic
4. Sports Illustrated article -April 10, 1978 *'Mavis, You're Just Amazing'*
   http://vault.sportsillustrated.cnn.com/vault/article/magazine/MAG1093516/index.htm
   Accessed: April 30, 08
5. Mavis Lindgren; *Who Is The Fastest, Oldest Female Marathoner?*
   http://diabetesdietdialogue.wordpress.com/2007/07/21/who-are-the-oldest-people-on-our-planet-and-why-are-they-that-healthy-part-5/

Accessed: April 30, 08

6. New York Times; *Marathon; At 86 Years Old, Mavis Lindgren is a Road Runner*
   http://query.nytimes.com/gst/fullpage.html?res=9F0CE2DA163AF93AA35752C1A965958260
   Accessed: April 30, 08

CHAPTER 12

1. http://en.wikipedia.org/wiki/Hudson_Taylor
   Accessed: May 16, 12
2. Tucker, Ruth (1983). *From Jerusalem to Irian Jaya A Biographical History of Christian Missions.* Grand Rapids, Michigan: Zondervan. p.73
3. The Educational Directory for China (1905), p.43
4. Christian Literature Society for China (1911), 281-282
5. God—I *listened—the Eula McClaney story*
6. http://www.lawattstimes.com/articles/2008/02/14/community/community4.txt
   Accessed: April 12, 08

CHAPTER 13

1. This aspect of the Biblical story of Michal is recorded in the Holy Bible 2 Samuel Chapter 6.
2. http://www.jsc.nasa.gov/Bios/htmlbios/chang.html
   Accessed: March 14, 08
3. http://www.infocostarica.com/people/franklin.html
   Accessed: March 14, 08
4. http://video.wired.com/?fr_story=4dba4602cbdf999fb6a786853e788ca46f59aa36&rf=rss

• NOTES •

Episode 107: Franklin Chang-Diaz Retired NASA astronaut and head of the Ad Astra Rocket Company, Franklin Chang-Diaz talks with special correspondent Adam Rogers about how his work is revolutionizing rocket engines. Accessed: April14, 08

4. http://www.adastrarocket.com/Franklin.html
    Accessed: March 30, 08

CHAPTER 14

1. http://www.beyondthelimits.com/about.shtml
    Accessed: April 14, 12
2. Allison, Stacy, Carlin, Peter, *Beyond the Limits: A Women's Triumph on Everest* (Bookpartners: 1999)

Stay connected!

Continue to find new strength to deliver more dreams!

Visit www.strengthtodeliver.com for more resources

www.ingramcontent.com/pod-product-compliance
Lightning Source LLC
Chambersburg PA
CBHW032102090426
42743CB00007B/210